Keiko Okamoto's
Japanese Knitting Stitches

A STITCH DICTIONARY WITH 150 AMAZING PATTERNS

Translated and introduced by
Gayle Roehm

TUTTLE Publishing

Tokyo | Rutland, Vermont | Singapore

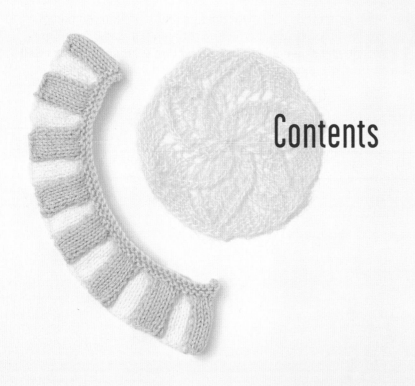

Contents

The following companies have contributed materials used in the making of the swatches and finished projects pictured in this book:

Clover Corporation
http://www.clover.co.jp
Daido International Puppy Division, Ltd.
http://www.puppyarn.com
Diamond Yarn Co. Ltd
http://www.diakeito.co.jp
Hamanaka Corporation
http://www.hamanaka.co.jp
Hamanaka Corporation Richmore Sales Dept.
http://www.richmore.jp
Motohiro Corporation
http://www.skiyarn.com
Naito Shoji Co., Ltd.
http://www.naitoshoji.co.jp
Yokota Corporation
http://www.daruma-ito.co.jp

9 Richmore Percent

About the author

If you pick up a Japanese knitting magazine or pattern collection, you're almost certain to find the work of Keiko Okamoto. She's one of Japan's best—known and most prolific hand knitting designers, and she works extensively with magazines, schools and yarn companies.

Based in Kobe, she is the proprietor of the K's K studio (http://atelier-ksk.net—Japanese only), which offers classes around Japan as well as her own line of yarn. She's interested in collaborations between knitting and techniques such as weaving, spinning, sewing and embroidery. This is her first published collection of knitting stitches.

If you thought all Japanese knitting was delicate lace, these unusual stitches will change your mind and challenge your skills. Okamoto has developed some extraordinarily innovative stitchwork. Some of these stitches are fairly conventional, some of them are quite challenging, and some are crazy fun. The book includes a few patterns for practice, then use your imagination.

Author's preface

Ancient literature tells us that knitting has come down to us from the bronze age. Now it's a familiar part of our existence. It's thought-provoking to consider that someone thousands of years ago did exactly what we're doing now.

Hand knitting is the process of making a surface with a single strand of yarn made into loops. Only hands and knitting needles are required. Within this simple manual work, a deep level of craft can be achieved. Knitting was born from practical necessity, and a wide variety of shapes and patterns have been added by ingenuity. Even though I repeat the same creative act, I've created countless patterns, and I'm very fond of them.

I've compiled many of my knitting patterns into this collection. It's a complement to my collection of crochet stitches that was released in 2012. To all of you who love knitting, I'll be truly happy if you keep this book in your hands.

Keiko Okamoto

Introduction

Be sure to read through this introduction before starting to knit. You'll find important information about interpreting the charts and symbols, identifying the pattern repeats, and using the stitch patterns in a knitted fabric.

Chart basics

To begin, you should be comfortable knitting from charts. Japanese designs don't provide stitch patterns in words. The chart-phobic knitter should probably give this book a pass.

Japanese charts normally don't provide a key for every chart, unlike Western patterns. The symbols are standardized, and every Japanese publisher uses the same symbol set. Therefore, a Japanese knitter is expected to know them. For Western knitters, we've added definitions for every symbol in the book, in the Symbol Directory on pages 128-135.

Your approach to a chart depends on whether you're working flat or in the round. If you're knitting back and forth:

- On the right side, read the chart from right to left, in the same sequence that you work the stitches.
- On the reverse (or "wrong") side, read the chart from left to right, and reverse the stitches, so that your stitches will show up correctly on the right side.
- Aside from knits and purls, not many stitches are worked on the wrong side. The Symbol Directory provides definitions for reverse side rows, if applicable. If only one definition is given, that particular symbol is only worked on right side rows.

If you're knitting in the round, read every row from right to left. There's no need to reverse stitches.

About the stitch symbols

The single most important thing to remember about working from charts is this: *the chart shows the right side of the work*. It's a visual representation of what your work will look like when it's done. Each symbol describes what the stitch will look like on the right side, not what you execute. For example, to create a knit stitch on the right side, you must purl on the reverse side. For these patterns, nothing too complicated is worked on the wrong side. Where appropriate, the Symbol Directory defines the wrong-side maneuvers.

As you work through the stitch patterns, you'll notice that the symbols look a lot like the stitches they represent. Just like the overall chart, the symbols are visual representations of what the stitch should look like; they're a sort of visual code. The symbol for knit 2 together, for instance, has two legs (two stitches are involved) and leans to the right (as the stitch does when complete). Basic stitch symbols may be combined, as well: knit 2 together with a "purl dash" (horizontal line) below it tells you to purl 2 together. Occasionally, a symbol may be elongated, like the k2togs at the top of pattern #85, to span a "no stitch" area.

Of the various stitch symbols in use around the world, the Japanese symbols look most like their corresponding stitches. As you get used to them, you'll probably wish all publishers would adopt this logical system. The Symbol Directory is cross-referenced to the stitch patterns that use each of the symbols, and many of them reference illustrations with more detailed explanations. There are also some variations or more complex symbols that are used in only one pattern. These are defined next to the appropriate chart.

For consistency, I've used the symbol definitions from Nihon Vogue, the original publisher, as found in *Knitting Symbol Book* (ISBN 978-4-529-05559-8).

Color patterns are keyed on each chart, using symbols different from those for stitches.

Crochet symbols

Okamoto has used a few crochet stitches as well—some as edgings, and many as crocheted bobbles. These are also defined in the Symbol Directory.

Blank boxes

For most of the charts, you'll see a number of blank boxes. Depending on the chart, a blank could mean a knit stitch, a purl stitch or a stockinette stitch. Before you start, check around the chart—usually in the lower left corner —to find the definition of the blank box.

☐ = K on RS, P on WS tells you that a blank box should look like a knit on the right side. This means it's purled on the wrong side. Lots of blank boxes indicate stockinette stitch.

☐ = P on RS, K on WS tells you that a blank box should look like a purl on the right side, so it's knit on the wrong side. Lots of blank boxes indicate stockinette stitch.

☐ = St st (in each color) indicates Stockinette stitch. You'll see this in many of the multicolored patterns.

This convention keeps the chart cleaner and easier to read—your eye can focus on what you have to do, without a lot of visual "noise" from the background stitches. Compare stitch patterns #13 and #14, for instance. Pattern #14 is based on stockinette stitch, while pattern #13 has a background of reverse stockinette.

Finding pattern repeats

This is a stitch dictionary, so you're encouraged to use it to design your own creations. It's important to understand how to find the repeat of a pattern when you want to use it across a larger piece of knitted fabric. Look for the stitch and row numbers to tell you what to repeat.

Row numbers are shown on the right hand side, and stitch numbers at the bottom. The rightmost column and the bottommost row are not stitches, but holders for those numbers.

Most charts begin in the lower right-hand corner. However, row 1 of the pattern repeat isn't necessarily the first row, and stitch 1 may not be the first stitch, so watch for your starting point. Not every chart includes edge stitches.

The charts for the edgings (patterns #131 to #150) don't specify the repeat in the same way, but the numbers at the bottom tell you which stitches to repeat.

A few of the unusual stitches have small sections worked back and forth, like the bobbles in pattern #116. Notice the small arrows on the bobble detail showing where the direction of knitting changes. The lace motifs (patterns #122 to #130) are variously worked center-out and outside-in. Pay close attention to the arrows in the schematic. Pattern #122, for instance, is worked outside-in with an edging worked out from the starting row.

Before you begin

Whether you want to make a complicated design, or just use a chart for a scarf, take these few steps to ensure that you understand the chart:

- Find the key that tells you whether a blank box is a knit or a purl. Keep in mind that this is how the stitch appears on the right side.
- Find the definitions for all the symbols included. This book contains both a Symbol Directory and some illustrations in the back, so you may need to look in more than one place.
- Find the marked stitch and row repeat. The stitch numbering across the bottom of the chart stops with the last stitch of the repeat. The row numbering up the right side stops with the last row of the repeat. That makes the repeat easy to spot. You may find it helpful to draw a heavy colored line around the repeat as a reminder, or to shade in that section of the chart.

About the patterns

There are seven patterns in the back of the book: three garments and four accessories. Each uses one of the stitch patterns as its inspiration.

To help you work the patterns, we've included:

- **Yarn data:** the name of the original yarn used, and approximate total yardage.
- Both metric and imperial measurements.
- Japanese, metric and U.S. needle and hook specifications.
- Additional explanations to supplement original text where needed.

The pattern format remains Japanese. Most of the instructions are presented graphically, as annotated schematics that tell you, for instance, how many stitches to cast on, as well as the finished measurements. This format may not be familiar, but you'll probably find it quite easy to follow.

Finally, the three garments are given in only one size, as is typical for a Japanese pattern. Pay close attention to the measurements on the schematic, and make adjustments where necessary to custom fit the design for yourself.

Yarn substitution

The yarns that were used for the stitches in this book are named at the top of each stitch pattern, along with the pattern number. These are Japanese yarns with limited availability in the US. Some are discontinued. To help with yarn substitution, we've provided a table of yarns used in the stitch patterns (p.7) and a table of yarns used in the projects in this book (p.102). Check the tables for weight, yardage, and fiber content (where known). In the case of yarns used in projects, if the yarn is listed on Ravelry, a link is given, where you may also find a photo.

Remember: whatever yarn you use, you should always swatch a stitch pattern in your chosen yarn to be sure you're happy with its look and feel. You'll also need an accurate gauge if you plan to knit a garment.

Yarn used	Type (app.)	Fiber content	Put-up
Clover Alpaca Mjuk	DK	80% alpaca, 20% acrylic	25g = 109y (100m)
Clover Champagne	Sport	60% wool, 20% angora, 15% nylon, 5% poly	25g = 110y (100m)
Clover Petit Fours	DK	100% wool	20g = 58y (53m)
Diakeito Tasmanian Merino	Sport	100% wool	40g = 131y (120m)
Diakeito Tasmanian Merino Tweed	DK	100% merino wool	40g = 131y (120m)
Hamanaka Arcoba	Fingering	90% wool, 4% other, 2% poly	25g = 110y (100m)
Hamanaka Etoffe	Aran	70% alpaca, 24% wool, 6% nylon	40g = 110y (100m)
Hamanaka Exceed Wool FL	Sport	100% merino wool	40g = 131y (120m)
Hamanaka Exceed Wool L	Worsted	100% merino wool	40g = 87y (80m)
Hamanaka Exceed Wool M	Fingering	100% merino wool	40g = 175y (167m)
Hamanaka Fair Lady 50	Worsted	70% wool, 30% acrylic	40g = 109y (100m)
Hamanaka Furish Gradation	Bulky	100% nylon	40g = 66y (60m)
Hamanaka Grand Etoffe	Super bulky	73% alpaca, 24% wool, 3% nylon	40g = 52y (48m)
Hamanaka Mohair Premier	Sport	55% mohair, 35% acrylic, 10% wool	25g = 98y (90m)
Hamanaka Organic Wool Field	Sport	100% wool	40g = 131y (120m)
Hamanaka Pure Wool Fingering	Fingering	100% wool	40g = 175y (160m)
Hamanaka Softy Tweed	Worsted	80% wool, 20% alpaca	40g = 103y (94m)
Hamanaka Sonomono Roving	Bulky	40% alpaca, 30% linen, 30% wool	40g = 69y (63m)
Hamanaka Sonomono Sport	Sport	100% wool	40g = 131y (120m)
Hamanaka Sonomono Tweed	DK	53% wool, 40% alpaca, 7% camel	40g = 120y (110m)
Hamanaka Span Tear	Fingering	68% poly, 13% mohair, 10% nylon, 9% wool	25g = 137y (125m)
Naito Shoji Alpaca Nazka	Worsted	100% alpaca	50g = 110y (100m)
Naito Shoji Alpaca Peru	Sport	100% alpaca	50g = 186yd (166m)
Naito Shoji Gaviano	Worsted	62% alpaca, 26% wool, 10% acrylic, 2% nylon	50g = 110y (100m)
Naito Shoji Lana Bio	Worsted	100% wool	50g = 131y (120m)
Naito Shoji Lana Bio Fine	Sport	100% wool	50g = 165m
Naito Shoji Zara	DK	100% wool	50g = 137y (125m)
Puppy New 4Ply	Fingering	100% wool	40g = 164y (150m)
Puppy Princess Anny	DK	100% wool	40g = 122y (112m)
Puppy Pure Silk	Sport	100% silk	40g = 160y (146m)
Puppy Queen Anny	Worsted	100% wool	50g = 106y (97m)
Puppy Shetland	DK	100% wool	40g = 98y (90m)
Puppy Silkid Fine	DK	55% mohair, 45% silk	25g = 120y (110m)
Richmore Percent	DK	100% wool	40g = 131y (120m)
Richmore Percent Gradation	DK	100% wool	(120m)
Richmore Soff Spark	Sport	48% merino, 20% alpaca, 16% nylon, 16% poly	25g = 88y (80m)
Richmore Spectre Modem	Aran	100% wool	40g = 87y (80m)
Richmore Suspense	Sport	66% rayon, 34% poly	25g = 115y (105m)
Richmore Teddy	Bulky	38% wool, 37% alpaca, 24% acrylic, 1% nylon	30g = 38y (35m)
Ski Cotton Gloss	Sport	100% cotton	40g = 154y (141m)
Ski Menuet	Worsted	100% wool	40g = 94y (86m)
Ski Nice	Worsted	65% poly, 35% cotton	30g = 127y (116m)
Ski Skiprimo Kuchen	Super bulky	100% wool	50g = 44y (40m)
Ski Sonata	DK	100% wool	40g = 131y (120m)

Overall Patterns

1 Richmore Percent

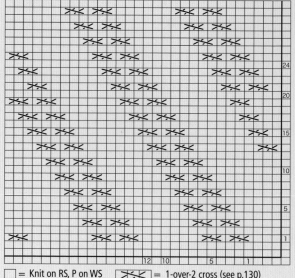

☐ = Knit on RS, P on WS   ✕✕ = 1-over-2 cross (see p.130)

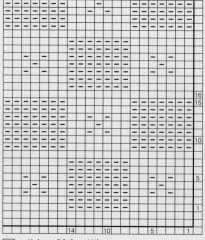

☐ = Knit on RS, P on WS

2 Naito Shoji Zara

3 Richmore Percent

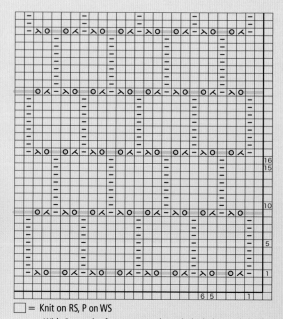

☐ = Knit on RS, P on WS

— = With 6 strands of yarn, weave through the holes made by the yarnovers.

4 Richmore Percent

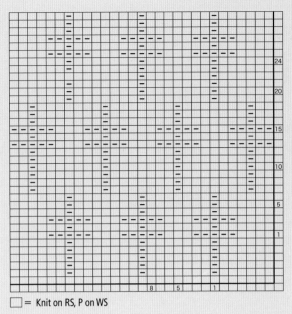

☐ = Knit on RS, P on WS

5 Diakeito Tasmanian Merino

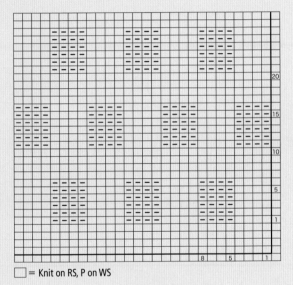

☐ = Knit on RS, P on WS

6 Naito Shoji Zara

☐ = Purl on RS, K on WS

7 Puppy Queen Anny

8 Diakeito Tasmanian Merino

☐ = Knit on RS,
P on WS

To work
this symbol

To work
this symbol

1) Knit st 1 ①
2) With tip of LN, pick up purl bump
   below st ① and knit it
1) With tip of RN, pick up the purl bump
   below st ②, place it on LN and knit it
2) Knit st ②

9 Richmore Percent

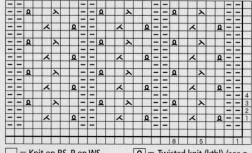

☐ = Knit on RS, P on WS   Ω = Twisted knit (ktbl) (see p. 129)

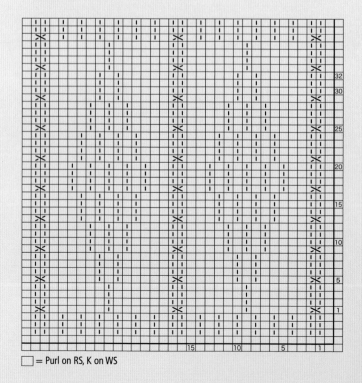

☐ = Purl on RS, K on WS

10 Hamanaka Sonomonono Tweed

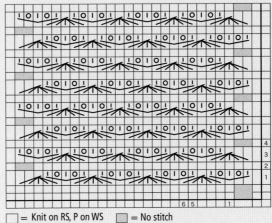

= Knit on RS, P on WS   = No stitch

To work this symbol
⑥⑤④③②①

1) Knit 5 together
2) Make 5 sts into next st by k, yo, k, yo, k
   (see p. 130)

11 (Chart on p. 45) Naito Shoji Lana Bio

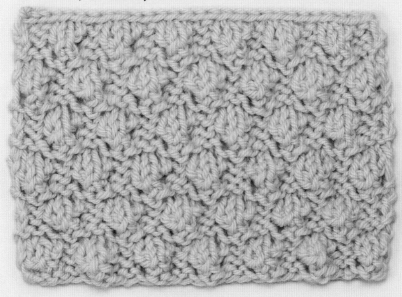

12 Diakeito Tasmanian Merino

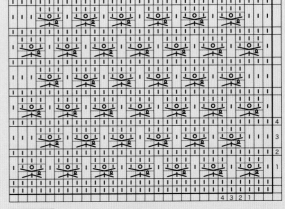

To work
this symbol
④③②①

1) K stitch ①
2) With sts ② to ④, work centered double
   decrease (see p. 129). Turn work.
3) On the wrong side, work ptbl, yo, ptbl into
   this stitch. Turn work.
4) On the right side, k3 into these 3 sts

13 Hamanaka Pure Wool Fingering

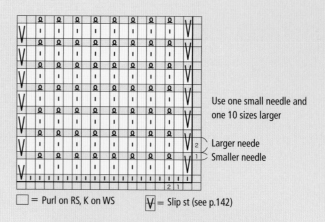

Use one small needle and
one 10 sizes larger

2 Larger neede
1 Smaller needle

☐ = Purl on RS, K on WS   Ⅴ = Slip st (see p.142)

14 Hamanaka Organic Wool Field

15 Ski Sonata

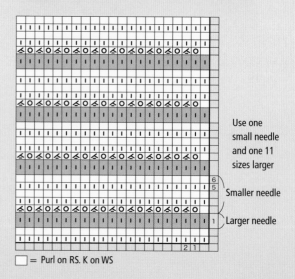

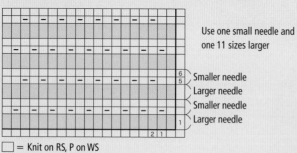

Use one small needle and
one 11 sizes larger

6
5 Smaller needle
   Larger needle
   Smaller needle
1 Larger needle

☐ = Knit on RS, P on WS

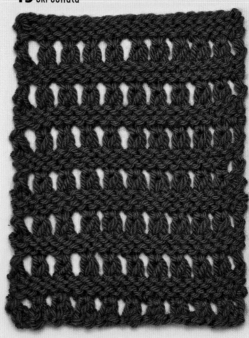

Use one
small needle
and one 11
sizes larger

6
5 Smaller needle

1 Larger needle

☐ = Purl on RS. K on WS

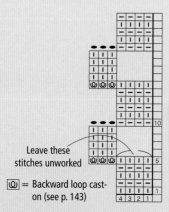

16 Clover Petits Fours

Leave these
stitches unworked

Ⓤ = Backward loop cast-
on (see p. 143)

17 (Chart on p. 104) **Naito Shoji Zara**

18 **Puppy Princess Anny**

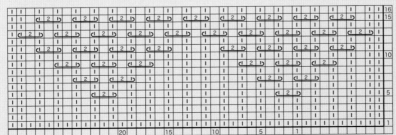

□ = Purl on RS, K on WS

⊂|2|⊃ = 2-stitch wrapped knot: k, p, k, then place these 3 sts on CN and wrap twice with working yarn (see 3-st wrapped knot on p. 143)

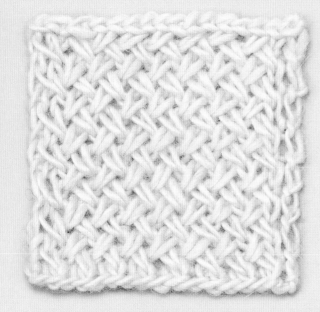

19 Richmore Percent

※On the last row, continue to cross stitches while binding off

20 Puppy Queen Anny

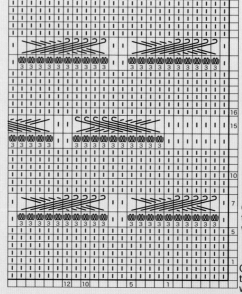

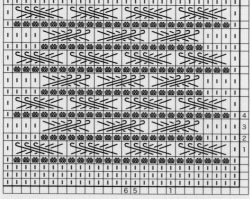

= Purl wrapping yarn twice around the needle (see p. 143)

= Cross 3 stitches through to the left (see p. 132)

= Cross 3 stitches through to the right (see p. 132)

21 Hamanaka Organic Wool Field

= Purl, wrapping yarn 3 times around needle (see p. 143)

= Cross 5 stitches through to the left (see p. 132, 3-st version)

= Cross 5 stitches through to the right (see p. 132, 3-st version)

22 Ski Skiprimo Kuchen

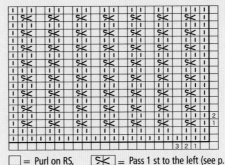

□ = Purl on RS, K on WS   ⟩⟨ = Pass 1 st to the left (see p. 132)

23 Naito Shoji Gaviano

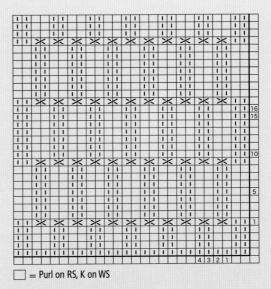

□ = Knit on RS, P on WS   ⟨⟨⟩ = Knit, wrapping yarn twice around the needle (see p. 143)

How to work these symbols

1) Slip 5 sts to RN, dropping extra wraps to make 5 elongated stitches. Return 5 st to LN. Without removing st from LN, [k5tog, yo] 4 times, k5tog to make 9 sts, then remove from LN.
2) On the next row, work 4 decreases as shown (p, [p2tog] 4x) to restore the stitch count to 5.

24 Naito Shoji Lana Bio Fine

□ = Purl on RS, K on WS

Smocking

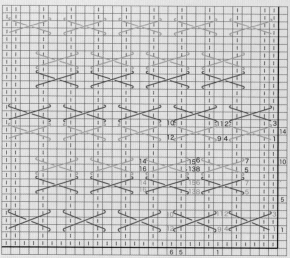

☐ = Purl on RS, K on WS — ‧ — ‧ — = Use Smocking yarn

※Work k1, p2 ribbing for the base fabric. With a separate strand of yarn in a contrasting color, work the smocking stitches. ※Place the smocking stitches over stitches and rows as shown on the chart. Small numbers in colored type show the path of the smocking stitch: bring smocking strand up at 1, down at 2, up at 3, down at 4; then up at 5, down at 6, and so on across the fabric, to bring ribbed stitches together. Pull the crossed stitches fairly tight.

26 Richmore Percent

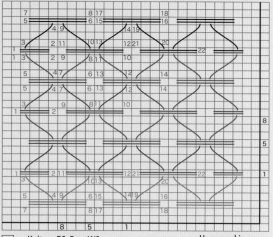

☐ = Knit on RS, P on WS — ‧ — ‧ — ‧ — = Use smocking yarn

※Work stockinette stitch for the base fabric. With a separate strand of yarn in a contrasting color, work the smocking stitches. Place the smocking stitches over stitches and rows as shown on the chart. Small numbers in colored type show the path of the smocking stitch: bring smocking strand up at 1, down at 2, up at 3, down at 4; then up at 5, down at 6, up at 7, down at 8, and so on across the fabric. Work the red rows of smocking first, following the numbers, then the blue rows, and so on. Horizontal smocking stitches have 2 strands, diagonal stitches have one.

27 Hamanaka Exceel Wool L

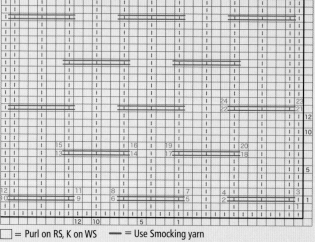

☐ = Purl on RS, K on WS — = Use Smocking yarn

※Work k1, p2 ribbing for the base fabric. With a separate strand of yarn in a contrasting color, work the smocking stitches. Place the smocking stitches over stitches and rows as shown on the chart. Small numbers in colored type show the path of the smocking stitch: bring smocking strand up at 1, down at 2, up at 3, down at 4, and so on across the fabric, to bring ribbed stitches together. Pull the crossed stitches fairly tight.

28 (Chart on p. 49) **Puppy Princess Anny**

29 Hamakaka Exceed Wool L

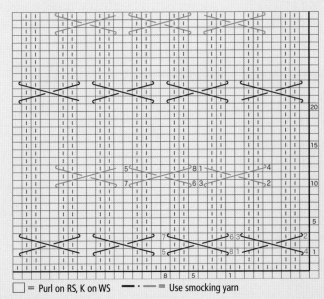

☐ = Purl on RS, K on WS   — · — = Use smocking yarn

※Work k2, p2 ribbing for the base fabric. With a separate strand of yarn in a contrasting color, work the smocking stitches. Place the smocking stitches over stitches and rows as shown on the chart. Small numbers in colored type show the path of the smocking stitch: bring smocking strand up at 1, down at 2, up at 3, down at 4; then up at 5, down at 6, and so on across the fabric, to bring ribbed stitches together. Pull the crossed stitches fairly tight.

30 (Chart on p. 40) Richmore Percent

31 Hamanaka Fair Lady 50

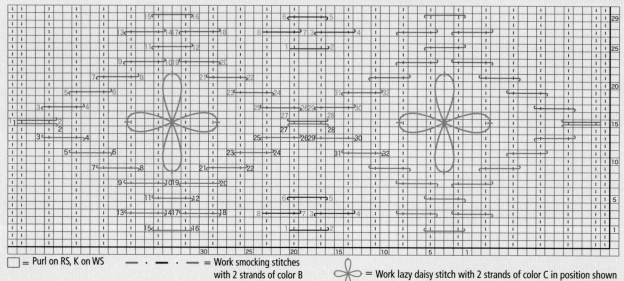

☐ = Purl on RS, K on WS　— - — · — = Work smocking stitches with 2 strands of color B　✣ = Work lazy daisy stitch with 2 strands of color C in position shown

※Work k1, p2 ribbing for the base fabric in color A. With 2 strands of yarn in color B, work the smocking stitches. Place the smocking stitches over stitches and rows as shown on the chart. Small numbers in colored type show the path of the smocking stitch in blue: bring smocking strand up at 1, down at 2, up at 3, down at 4; then up at 5, down at 6, up at 7, and down at 8. With another 2 strands of color B, begin again at 1 (on the left), and follow the green smocking path across the fabric. Repeat for the stitches in red. (Although the photo shows smocking in one color, the colors on the chart clarify the sequence in which to work smocking stitches.)

32 Richmore Percent

□ = Knit (in each color)	□ = Color A □ = Color B
— = Smocking stitch with 2 strands of color C
— = Smocking stitch with 2 strands of color D

※Work the base fabric in 2 colors as charted: 4 rows of stockinette in color A, followed by k2 rows, p2 rows in color B (if working back and forth). (The first cast-on row in color A is not shown on the chart.) Smocking stitches are worked vertically with contrast yarn. Small numbers in colored type show the path of the smocking stitch. Start with 2 strands of yarn in color B, and bring smocking strand up at 1, down at 2, up at 3, down at 4, and so on across the fabric, so the rows of purl stitches come together. Work the purple rows of smocking first, following the numbers, then the blue rows, and so on. (Although the photo shows smocking in one color, the colors on the chart clarify the sequence in which to work smocking stitches.)

33 (Chart on p. 41) Richmore Percent

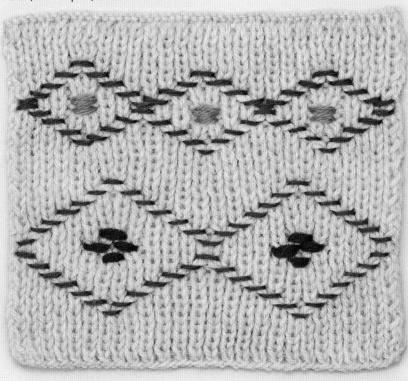

Openwork Stitches

34 Puppy Silkid Fine

35 Hamanaka Exceed Wool M

☐ = Knit on RS, P on WS

36 Puppy Shetland

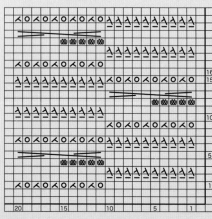

☐ = Knit on RS, p on WS

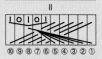

☐ = Knit on RS, P on WS

▥ = Purl, wrapping yarn twice
around needle

⅄ How to work these symbols

1) Insert RN below the purl bump of the row below st ①;
knit it, without removing from LN
2) Knit st ①
3) Pass st ① over st ②

How to work
these symbols

1) Slip sts ① to ⑤ to CN, dropping extra wraps. Hold to front.
2) Knit sts ⑥ to ⑩
3) Slip 5 sts on CN back to LN. K5togtbl; without removing from LN,
[yo, k5togtbl] twice more into the same sts

20

37 Richmore Spectre Modem

38 (Chart on p. 35) **Richmore Percent**

□ = Knit on RS, P on WS

= Twisted knit crossed to the left (see p. 139)

= Twisted knit crossed to the left (see p. 139)

★= On the last row, remove this stitch from the needle and let it drop down
※When binding off, bind off the top strand of the dropped st as one st.

39 Hamanaka Exceed Wool L

40 Puppy Shetland

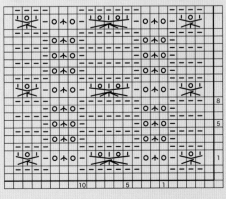

□ = Knit on RS, P on WS

How to work
these symbols

1) Knit 3 together.
2) Without removing the stitch from LN, yarn over and knit the same 3 sts together again. (see p. 138) The 5-stitch version is worked in the same way: [knit 5 tog, yo] twice, knit 5 tog.

Knit on RS,
□ = P on WS

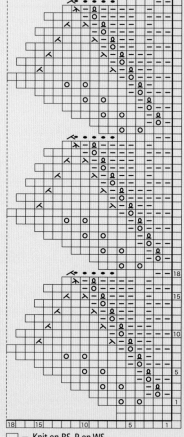

$\square$ = Knit on RS, P on WS

42 Hamanaka Exceed Wool FL

---

43 continued from p. 23

With color B and crochet hook, [chain 3, then chain 1, catching 4 strands from dropped stitches], repeat to end. (Chain 2 on first and last repeat.)

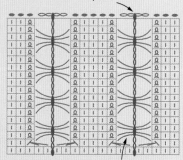

Strands of dropped stitches

45 continued from p. 23

How to work these symbols:

1) Yarn over, bring the right needle in front of stitch ①, and knit st ② , leaving both on LN.
2) Slip st ① to RN, let st ② drop from LN.
3) Return st ① to LN, k2tog with st ③ .

43 Clover Champagne and Petit Fours

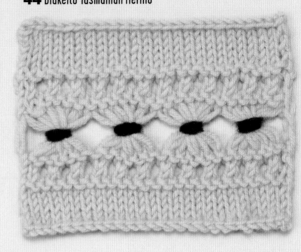

How to work these symbols
③ ② ①
1) With stitches ① to ③, slip 1, k2tog, psso.
2) Yarn over. 1 stitch decreased.

How to work these symbols
③ ② ①
1) Yarn over.
2) With stitches ① to ③, k3tog. 1 stitch decreased.

※Work the base fabric in color A.
※At the ★ (last row), let these 2 stitches drop off needle and ladder down.
※For the last row, bind off with a crochet hook and chain 4 over the space above the dropped stitches.
See p. 22 for how to chain up over the dropped stitches.

☐ = Knit on RS, P on WS
⟨ⓦ⟩ = (Worked on WS) Purl, wrapping yarn 4 times around needle. On the next row: k1, dropping extra wraps; place 3 sts on CN, dropping extra wraps, and hold to front; k3, dropping extra wraps; k3 from CN.

With color B, wrap 4 times around the 6 stitches of the cable crossing. Use a separate strand of yarn for each wrap, cutting yarn and reattaching each time.

※Work the base fabric in color A.

44 Diakeito Tasmanian Merino

45 Naito Shoji Zara

☐ = Knit on RS, P on WS

⟨⟩ See p. 22 for this symbol.

46 Richmore Percent

Knit on RS,
☐ = P on WS

Color Changing Patterns

47 Diakeito Tasmanian Merino

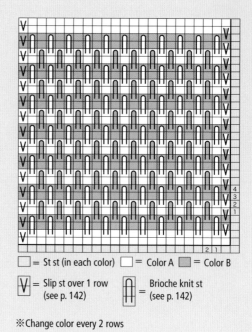

☐ = St st (in each color) ☐ = Color A ▧ = Color B

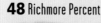= Slip st over 1 row (see p. 142)   ⊓ = Brioche knit st (see p. 142)

※Change color every 2 rows

48 Richmore Percent

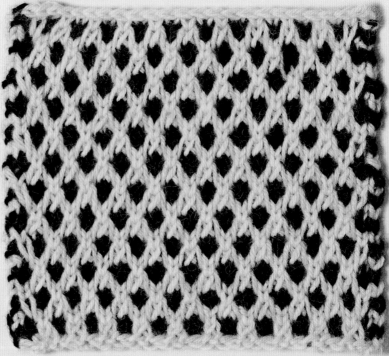

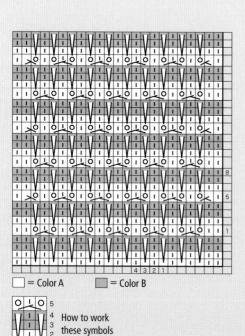

☐ = Color A   ▧ = Color B

How to work these symbols

1) Row 1 (RS): Knit with color A.
2) Row 2 (WS): With color A, slip wyif st ①, p st ②, slip wyif st ③.
3) Row 3 (RS): Change to color B. Slip wyib st ① k st ②, slip wyib st ③.
4) Row 4 (WS): With color B, slip wyif st ①, p st ②, slip wyif. st ③.
5) Row 5 (RS): Change to color A. Yo, then with RN, go in front of st ② and pick up st ③, then st ①, and take st ① off LN. Knit st ② and take sts ② and ③ off LN. Pass sts ① and ③ over st ②, then yo. Repeat rows 2 – 5.

※Change colors every 2 rows.

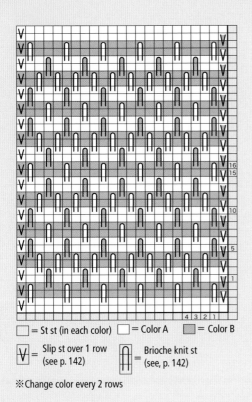

☐ = St st (in each color) ☐ = Color A ▨ = Color B

Ⓥ = Slip st over 1 row (see p. 142) ⋒ = Brioche knit st (see, p. 142)

※Change color every 2 rows

49 Hamanaka Organic Wool Field

50 Richmore Percent

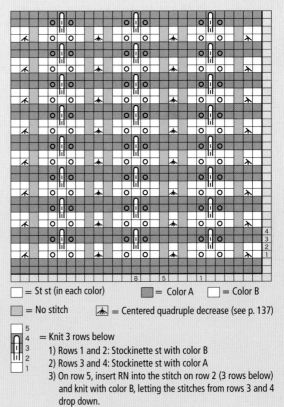

☐ = St st (in each color) ▨ = Color A ☐ = Color B

▨ = No stitch ⋔ = Centered quadruple decrease (see p. 137)

⋒ = Knit 3 rows below

1) Rows 1 and 2: Stockinette st with color B
2) Rows 3 and 4: Stockinette st with color A
3) On row 5, insert RN into the stitch on row 2 (3 rows below) and knit with color B, letting the stitches from rows 3 and 4 drop down.

※Change color every 2 rows

51 (Chart on p. 48) Richmore Percent

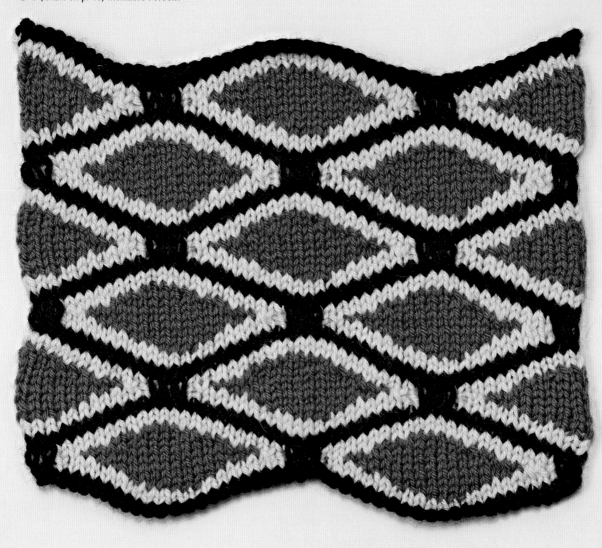

52 (Chart on p. 27) Hamanaka Exceed Wool FL

53 Hamanaka Grand Etoffe, Fair Lady 50, Furish (Gradation), Softy Tweed, Mohair Premier

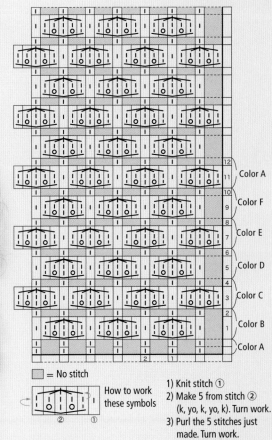

Color A
Color B
Color A
Color F
Color E
Color D
Color C
Color B
Color A

☐ = No stitch

How to work these symbols

1) Knit stitch ①
2) Make 5 from stitch ②
   (k, yo, k, yo, k). Turn work.
3) Purl the 5 stitches just made. Turn work.
4) Work centered quadruple decrease (see p. 129).

52 (See photo on p. 26)

54 (Chart on p. 48) Diakeito Tasmanian Merino, Tasmanian Merino Tweed

Work the sections on each side of the heavy line separately.

Work the sections on each side of the heavy line separately.

Work the sections on each side of the heavy line separately.

With color B, wrap these 2 rows 5 times.

● = Attach yarn
● = Cut yarn
※ Work main sections in color A

55 Puppy New 4Ply

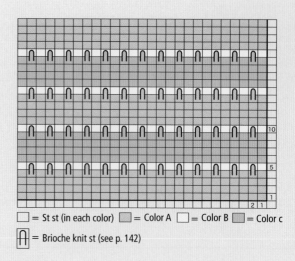

◻ = St st (in each color)   ▩ = Color A   ◻ = Color B   ▨ = Color c

⋔ = Brioche knit st (see p. 142)

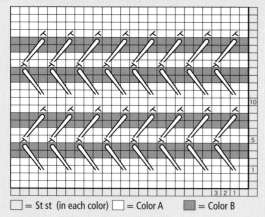

◻ = St st (in each color)   ◻ = Color A   ▩ = Color B

How to work these symbols

1) Work rows 1–4 in stockinette.
2) On row 5, knit sts ① and ②. On st ③, use the tip of RN to lift the loop of stitch ① from row 1, and place it on LN. SSK with the next stitch on LN.
3) Work rows 6 to 8 in stockinette.
4) On st ① of row 9, pick up the loop of st ③ from row 5, place it on LN, and k2tog with next st on LN. K sts ② and ③.

56 Puppy Princess Anny

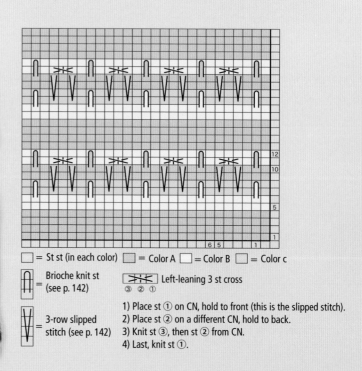

◻ = St st (in each color)   ▩ = Color A   ◻ = Color B   ▨ = Color c

⋔ = Brioche knit st (see p. 142)

✕ = Left-leaning 3 st cross

1) Place st ① on CN, hold to front (this is the slipped stitch).
2) Place st ② on a different CN, hold to back.
3) Knit st ③, then st ② from CN.
4) Last, knit st ①.

57 Puppy New 4Ply

Ⅴ = 3-row slipped stitch (see p. 142)

58 Ski Nice, Cotton Gloss

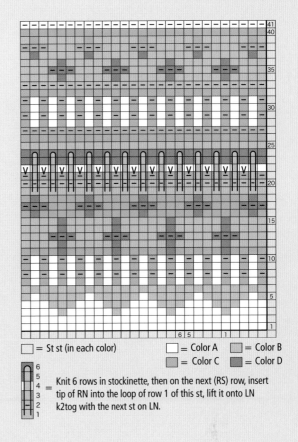

☐ = St st (in each color) ☐ = Color A ▨ = Color B

▨ = Color C ▨ = Color D

= Knit 6 rows in stockinette, then on the next (RS) row, insert tip of RN into the loop of row 1 of this st, lift it onto LN k2tog with the next st on LN.

59 Pupply Pure Silk

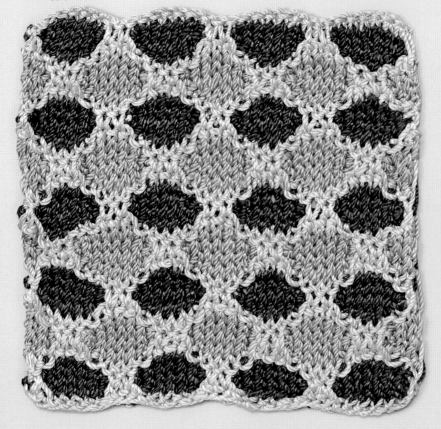

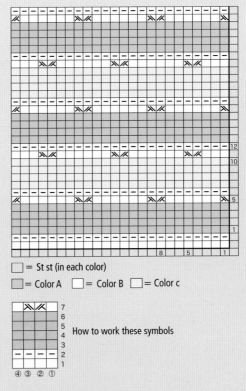

☐ = St st (in each color)

☐ = Color A ☐ = Color B ☐ = Color c

How to work these symbols

1) Work rows 1 to 6 as charted. On row 7, knit st ①.
2) On st ②, with tip of RN, pick up from row 1 the purl bumps of sts ② and ① in that order, placing them on RN. K st ②, and pass the 2 picked-up loops over it.
3) On st ③, with tip of RN, pick up from row 1 the purl bumps of of sts ③ and ④ in that order, placing them on RN. K st ③, and pass the 2 picked-up loops over it. K st ④.

60 Clover Petits Fours

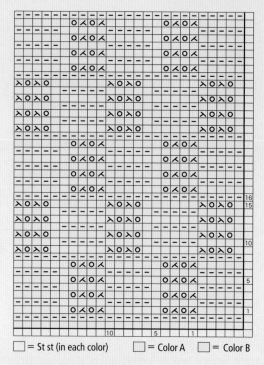

☐ = St st (in each color)　　☐ = Color A　　☐ = Color B

61 (Chart on p. 67) Richmore Percent

62 Clover Petits Fours

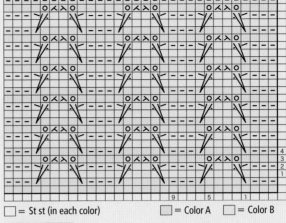

☐ = St st (in each color)　　☐ = Color A　　☐ = Color B

How to work these symbols

1) Row 1 in color B (RS): Slip sts ① and ⑥ wyib, knit the others.
2) Row 2 in color B (WS):): Change positions of sts ① and ② on LN so that ① crosses behind ②, then purl them. P sts ③ and ④; change positions of sts ⑤ and ⑥ on LN so that ⑥ crosses behind ⑤, then purl them.
3) Row 3 (RS) in color A: K, yo, ssk, k2tog, yo, k. Next row, change to color A and purl all sts.

63 Richmore Percent

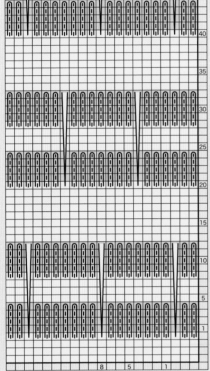

☐ = St st (in each color)

▯ = 4-row tuck st (see p. 143)

∨ = Slip over 12 rows

☐ = Color A
☐ = Color B
☐ = Color C

64 Richmore Percent

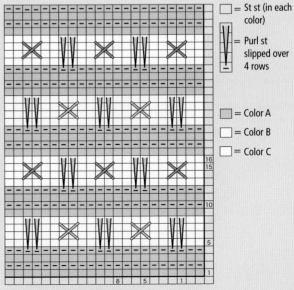

☐ = St st (in each color)

∨ = Purl st slipped over 4 rows

☐ = Color A
☐ = Color B
☐ = Color C

✖ = Cross stitch in color D or color E

Stranded Patterns

65 (Chart on p. 34) Richmore Percent

66 (Chart on p. 34) Richmore Percent

67 (Chart on p. 35) Richmore Percent

68 (Chart on p. 34) Richmore Percent

65 (See photo on p. 32)

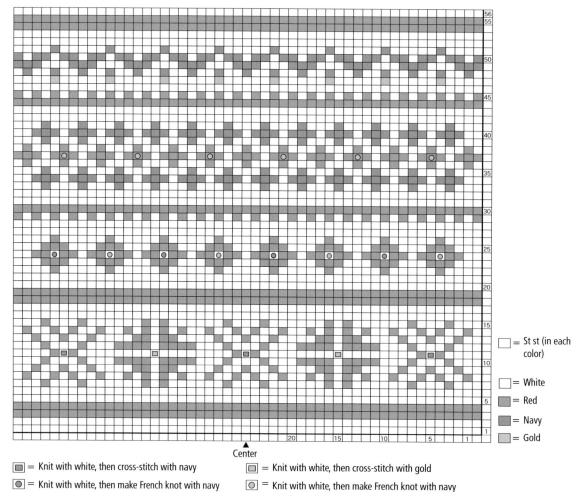

▲
Center

□ = St st (in each color)

□ = White

▨ = Red

■ = Navy

▨ = Gold

▨ = Knit with white, then cross-stitch with navy   ▨ = Knit with white, then cross-stitch with gold

◉ = Knit with white, then make French knot with navy   ◉ = Knit with white, then make French knot with navy

◉ = Knit with red, then make French knot with gold

66 (See photo on p. 32)

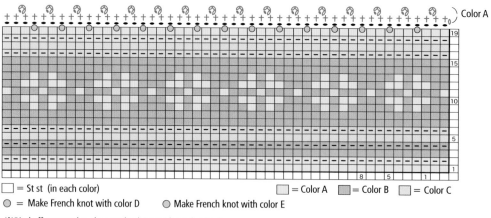

⟩ Color A

□ = St st (in each color)   □ = Color A   ▨ = Color B   □ = Color C

○ = Make French knot with color D   ● Make French knot with color E

※ Bind off at top edge, then work edging with crochet hook

68 (See photo on p. 33)

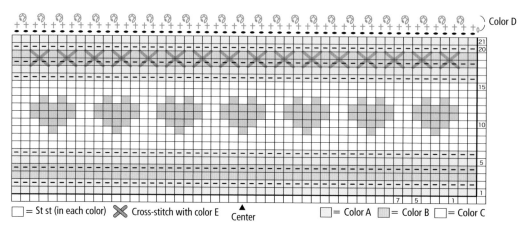

⟩ Color D

▲
Center

□ = St st (in each color)   ✕ Cross-stitch with color E   □ = Color A   ▨ = Color B   □ = Color C

34

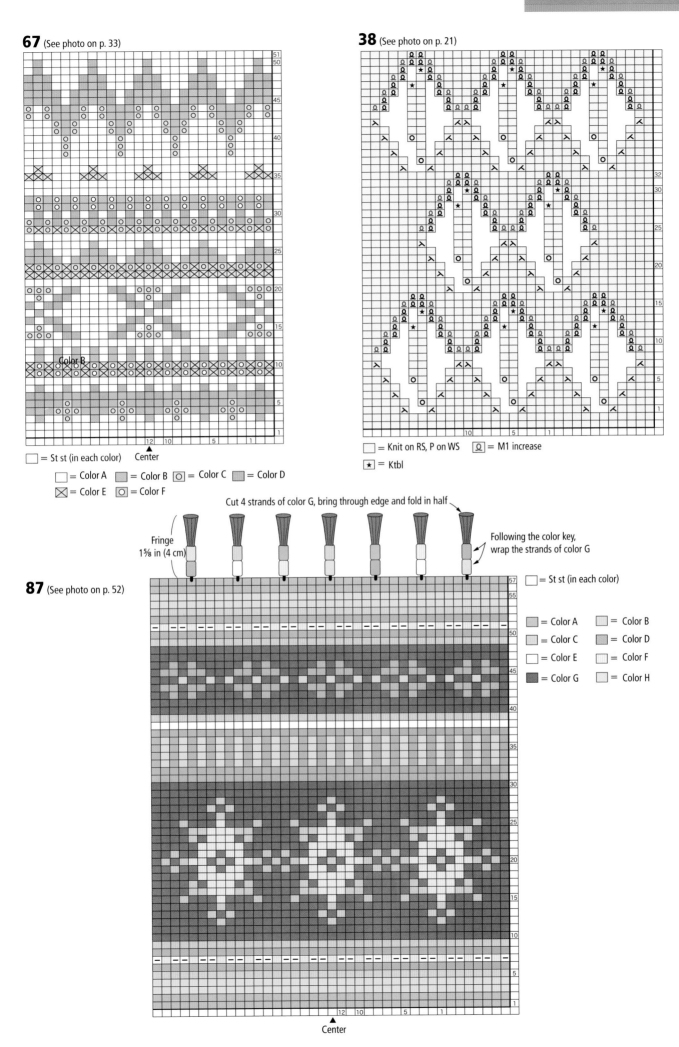

67 (See photo on p. 33)

38 (See photo on p. 21)

□ = St st (in each color)   ▲ Center

□ = Color A   ▨ = Color B   ⊡ = Color C   ▨ = Color D

⊠ = Color E   ⊡ = Color F

□ = Knit on RS, P on WS   Ω = M1 increase

★ = Ktbl

Cut 4 strands of color G, bring through edge and fold in half

Fringe 1⅝ in (4 cm)

Following the color key, wrap the strands of color G

87 (See photo on p. 52)

□ = St st (in each color)

▨ = Color A   □ = Color B

▨ = Color C   ▨ = Color D

□ = Color E   □ = Color F

▨ = Color G   □ = Color H

▲ Center

69 (Chart on p. 37) Richmore Percent

70 (Chart on p. 37) Richmore Percent

69 (See photo on p. 36)

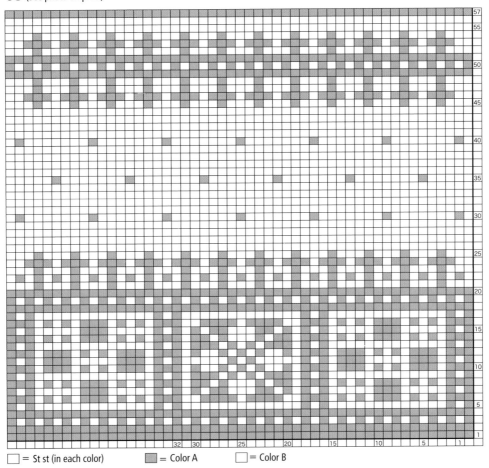

☐ = St st (in each color)   ▨ = Color A   ☐ = Color B

70 (See photo on p. 36)

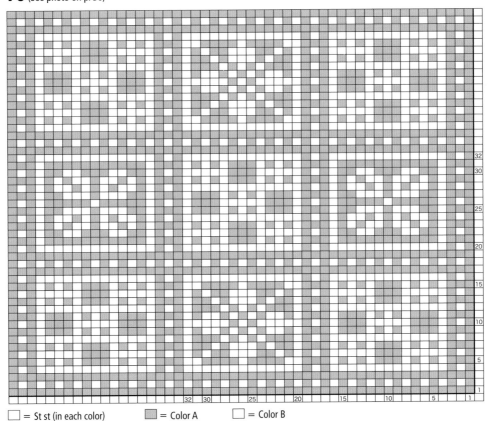

☐ = St st (in each color)   ▨ = Color A   ☐ = Color B

72 (Chart on p. 41) Richmore Percent

71

(See photo on p. 38)

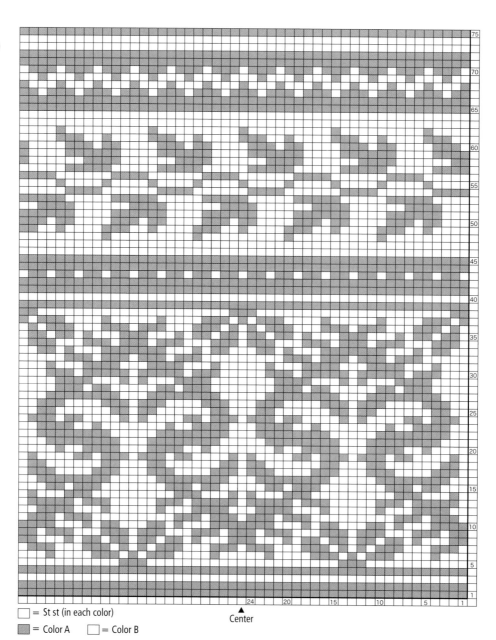

☐ = St st (in each color)

▦ = Color A   ☐ = Color B

▲ Center

30

(See photo on p. 18)

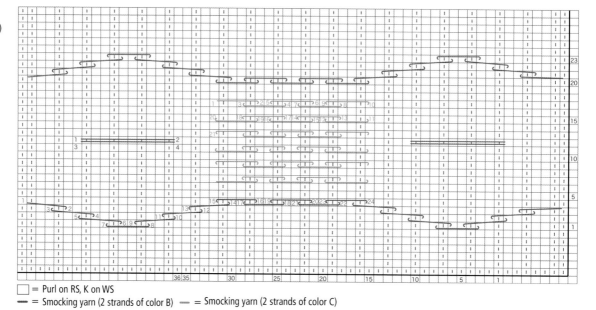

☐ = Purl on RS, K on WS

— = Smocking yarn (2 strands of color B)   — = Smocking yarn (2 strands of color C)

※Work k1, p2 ribbing for the base fabric in color A. With 2 strands of yarn in color B, work the smocking stitches. Place the smocking stitches over stitches and rows as shown on the chart. Small numbers in colored type show the path of the smocking stitch in blue: bring smocking strand up at 1, down at 2, up at 3, down at 4; then up at 5, down at 6, up at 7, down at 8 and so on. With another 2 strands of color B, begin again at 1 (on the left), and work the 2 smocking sections at left and right. With 2 strands in color C, repeat for the stitches in red.

72 (See photo on p. 39)

□ = St st (in each color) ▲ Center ■ = Color A □ = Color B

33 (See photo on p. 19)

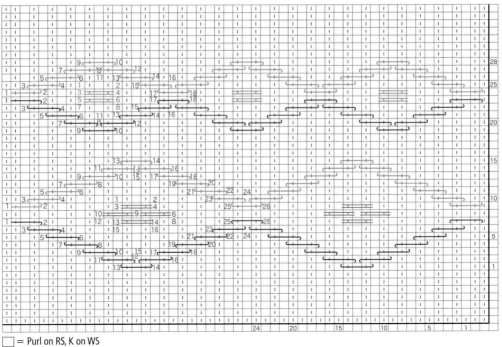

□ = Purl on RS, K on WS

— · — = Smocking yarn in color B   ▬ = Smocking yarn in color C   — = Smocking yarn in color D

※Work k1, p2 ribbing for the base fabric in color A. With yarn in color B, work the smocking stitches. Place the smocking stitches over stitches and rows as shown on the chart. Small numbers in colored type show the path of the smocking stitch in blue: bring smocking strand up at 1, down at 2, up at 3, down at 4; then up at 5, down at 6, up at 7, down at 8, and so on for the lower section. With another strand of color B, begin again at 1 (on the left), and follow the upper smocking path across the fabric. With yarn in color C, repeat for the smocking stitches in the centers of the diamonds.

73 (Chart on p. 44) Richmore Percent

74 Richmore Percent

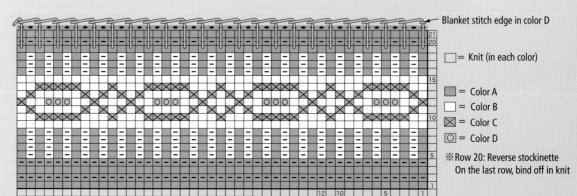

→ Blanket stitch edge in color D

☐ = Knit (in each color)

■ = Color A
☐ = Color B
☒ = Color C
◻ = Color D

※ Row 20: Reverse stockinette
On the last row, bind off in knit

75 (Chart on p. 45) Richmore Percent

76 (Chart on p. 45) Richmore Percent

73 (See photo on p. 42)

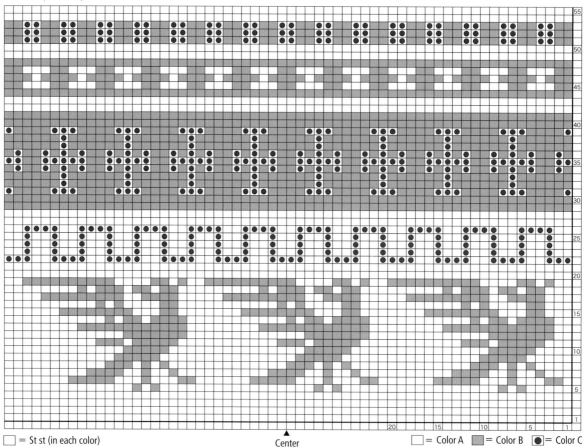

☐ = St st (in each color)

▲
Center

☐ = Color A ▨ = Color B ⬤ = Color C

81 (See photo on p. 47)

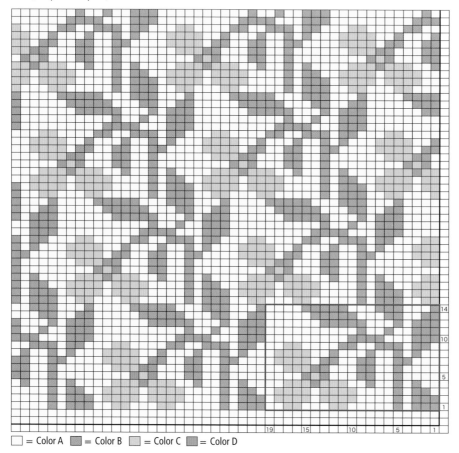

☐ = Color A ▨ = Color B ☐ = Color C ▨ = Color D

※All rows stockinette stitch
※Pattern repeat is outlined in red. ☐ One repeat = 19 stitches and 14 rows. After each 14-row repeat, move pattern 4 stitches to the left.

75
(See photo on p. 43)

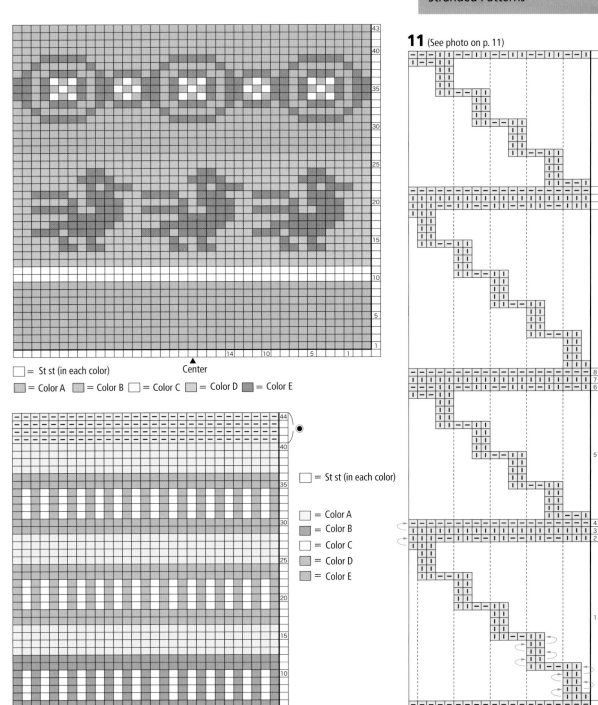

Center

☐ = St st (in each color)

▨ = Color A ▨ = Color B ☐ = Color C ▨ = Color D ▨ = Color E

11 (See photo on p. 11)

76
(See photo on p. 43)

☐ = St st (in each color)

☐ = Color A
▨ = Color B
☐ = Color C
▨ = Color D
▨ = Color E

※ ◉ = Using all colors but A, cut strands of yarn about 5cm (2") long. To work into the edge, tie a cut strand to yarn A, knit 2 with A, then move the tied strand to the front side of the knit fabric and knit 2 more with A. Use colors in random order as you please. When you feel that you're finished, trim all the strands to the same length.
※ Bind off on the last row

93
(See photo on p. 54)

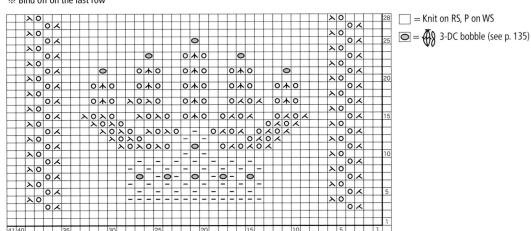

☐ = Knit on RS, P on WS

◉ = 3-DC bobble (see p. 135)

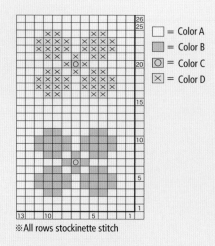

	= Color A
▨	= Color B
⦿	= Color C
⊠	= Color D

※All rows stockinette stitch

78 Richmore Percent

77 (Chart on p. 48) **Richmore Percent**

79 (Chart on p. 49)
Richmore Percent

81 (Chart on p. 44) **Richmore Percent**

80 Richmore Percent

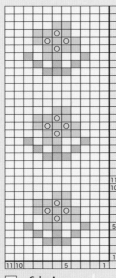

☐ = Color A
▨ = Color B
▧ = Color C
Ⓞ = Color D

※All rows stockinette stitch

82 Richmore Percent

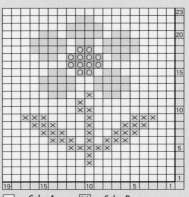

☐ = Color A   ☒ = Color B
▧ = Color C   Ⓞ = Color D

※All rows stockinette stitch

51 (See photo on p. 26)

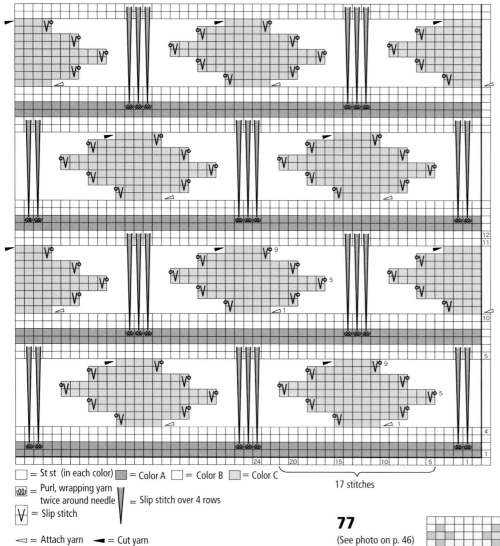

□ = St st (in each color) ▨ = Color A □ = Color B ▨ = Color C

⊚ = Purl, wrapping yarn twice around needle ▼ = Slip stitch over 4 rows

V̲ = Slip stitch

◁ = Attach yarn ◀ = Cut yarn

17 stitches

77

(See photo on p. 46)

□ = Color A ▨ = Color B ▨ = Color C ▨ = Color D

※All rows stockinette stitch

54 (See photo on p. 27)

17 stitches

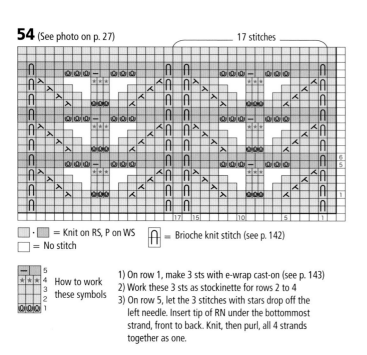

▨ · ▨ = Knit on RS, P on WS

□ = No stitch

∩ = Brioche knit stitch (see p. 142)

How to work these symbols

1) On row 1, make 3 sts with e-wrap cast-on (see p. 143)
2) Work these 3 sts as stockinette for rows 2 to 4
3) On row 5, let the 3 stitches with stars drop off the left needle. Insert tip of RN under the bottommost strand, front to back. Knit, then purl, all 4 strands together as one.

89 (See photo on p. 53)

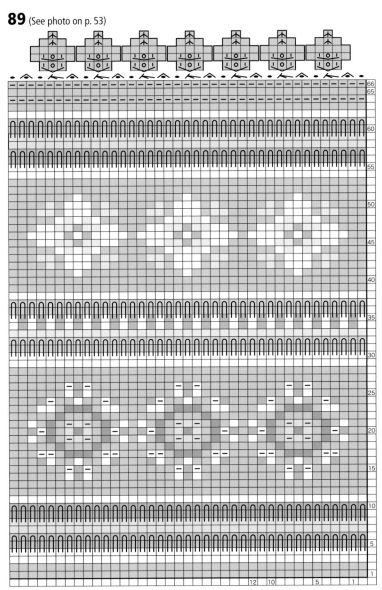

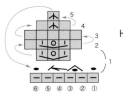

How to work these symbols

1) Row 1: knit st ①.
2) Now k2tog with sts ② and ③, then pass st ① over. Return st ② to LN.
3) Using sts ②, ④, and ⑤, k3tog, yo, k3tog again in the same stitches (see p. 138). Turn work.
4) Row 2 (WS): purl, yo, purl, yo, purl. Turn work.
5) Row 3 (RS): knit 5. Turn work.
6) Row 4 (WS): purl, centered double decrease (see p. 129), purl. Turn work.
7) Row 5 (RS): Centered double decrease.(see p. 137).
8) To continue: knit st ⑥ and pass the CDD over it. Continue to next motif, working from step 2 above.

▨ = Color A   ☐ = Color B   ▨ = Color C   ▨ = Color D

▨ = Color E   ▨ = Color F   ▨ = Color G   ☐ = Color H

☐ = St st (in each color)

⋔ = 3- row tuck stitch (see p. 143 for 6-row version).

28 (See photo on p. 17)

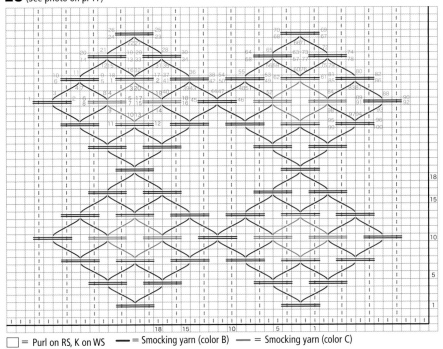

☐ = Purl on RS, K on WS   ▬▬ = Smocking yarn (color B)   ▬▬ = Smocking yarn (color C)

※With yarn in color B, work the smocking stitches shown in blue. Place the smocking stitches over stitches and rows as shown on the chart. Small numbers in colored type show the path of the smocking stitch in blue: bring smocking strand up at 1, down at 2, up at 3, down at 4; then up at 5, down at 6, up at 7, down at 8, and so on for the lower section. With another strand of color B, begin again at 1 (on the left), and follow the upper smocking path across the fabric. With yarn in color C, repeat for the smocking stitches in the centers of the diamonds.
※The numbers in color show the smocking stitch sequence. Use color as indicated.

79 (See photo on p. 46)

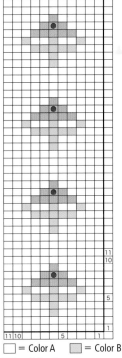

☐ = Color A   ▨ = Color B

▨ = Color C

⊙ = After knitting with color C, work a French knot with color D

※Al rows stockinette stitch

83 Richmore Percent

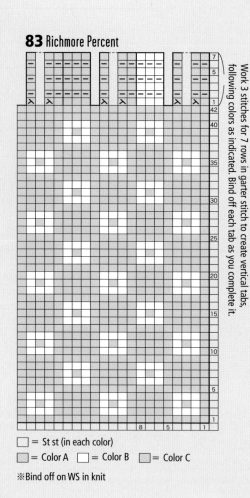

Work 3 stitches for 7 rows in garter stitch to create vertical tabs, following colors as indicated. Bind off each tab as you complete it.

☐ = St st (in each color)

☐ = Color A ☐ = Color B ☐ = Color C

※Bind off on WS in knit

84 Richmore Percent

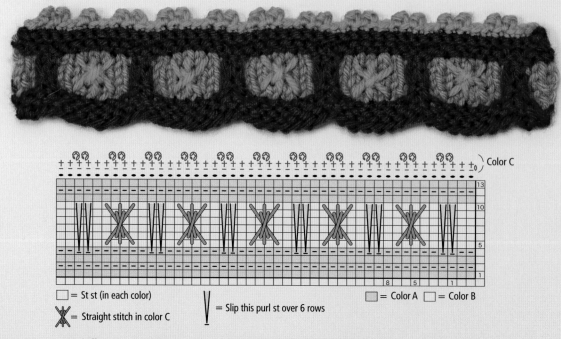

Color C

☐ = St st (in each color)   ☐ = Color A ☐ = Color B

✕ = Straight stitch in color C   V = Slip this purl st over 6 rows

※Bind off on WS in knit. Work sc into the back half of the loop of each bound off stitch.

85 Richmore Percent

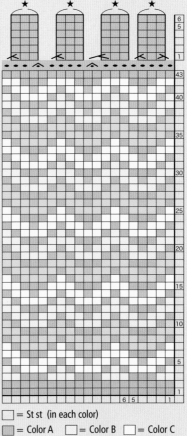

☐ = St st (in each color)

☐ = Color A   ☐ = Color B   ☐ = Color C

☐ = Color D   ☐ = Color E

※When stranded section is complete, bind off in knit on WS, decreasing at the points shown. Leave last st on RN; don't break yarn. Pick up sts from back loop of bound-off stitches, and work the tabs as charted, one at a time. On the last row (marked with ★), bind off the last 3 sts by picking up the purl bump from behind the same st in row 1, k2tog, and bind off. Continue to the next tab.

86 Richmore Percent

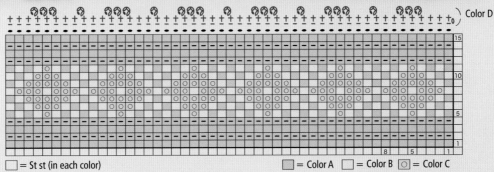

☐ = St st (in each color)   ☐ = Color A   ☐ = Color B   ☐ = Color C

※Except for the purls and the edging in color D, work in stockinette.
※When the stranded section is complete, bind off in knit on WS.
※Work sc into the back half of the loop of each bound off stitch.

88 Richmore Percent

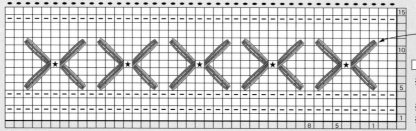

Work straight stitch with 1 strand of each of 3 colors.

☐ = Knit on RS, P on WS

※Work base fabric in color A. Work straight stitches are colors B, C and D.
※Bind off from WS in knit.
※Pass the embroidery strands under this stitch (marked with ★).

89 (Chart on p. 49) Richmore Percent

90 Richmore Percent

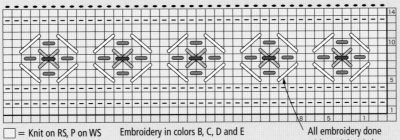

☐ = Knit on RS, P on WS   Embroidery in colors B, C, D and E

All embroidery done with straight stitches.

※Work base fabric in color A. Bind off from RS in purl.

Patterns with Bobbles

91 Hamanaka Organic Wool Field

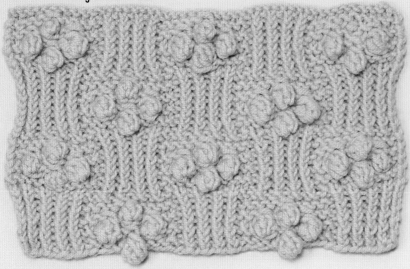

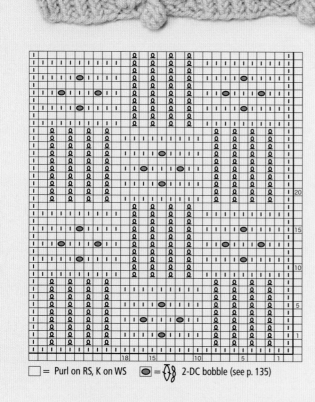

□ = Purl on RS, K on WS ● = 2-DC bobble (see p. 135)

92 (Chart on p. 106) Richmore Percent

93 (Chart on p. 45) Richmore Percent

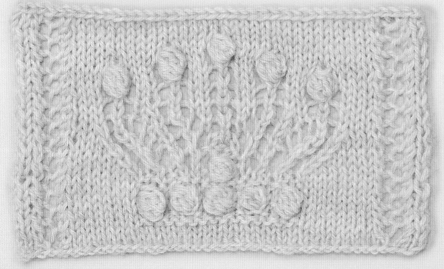

94 Richmore Percent

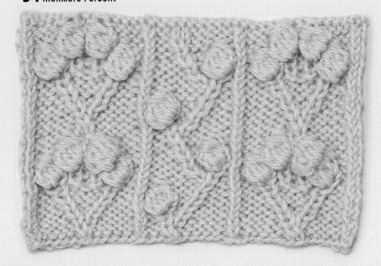

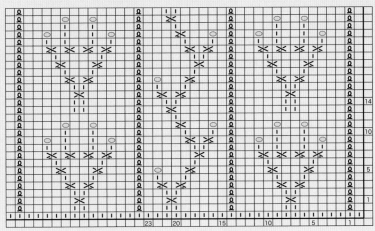

☐ = Purl on RS, K on WS

⧓ = Cross to the left over purl (see p. 139)

⧓ = Cross to the right over purl (see p. 139)

◯ = 4-DC bobble (see p. 135)

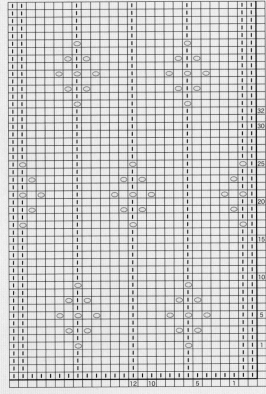

95 Richmore Percent

☐ = Purl on RS, K on WS

◯ = 3-DC bobble (see p. 135)

Patterns with Crossing Stitches

96 (Chart on p. 58) **Puppy Queen Anny**

97 Puppy Queen Anny

□ = Purl on RS, K on WS

7 stitches = 1 pattern repeat

→ Cast on stitches

※Cast on with crochet hook as shown (chain and bobbles).
※With knitting needle, pick up stitches for row 1 from the back loop of each chain.
※Bind off from RS in knit.

How to work

1) Chain 4, then chain 3 to begin bobble.
2) Work 2-DC bobble into half of the loop and back bump of the 4th chain from hook.
3) Chain 2, slip st to 4th chain, then continue with chain 7.

98 (Chart on pp. 58-59) *Ski Sonata*

99 *Ski Sonata*

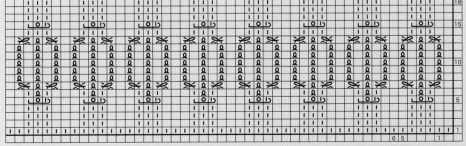

☐ = Purl on RS, K on WS   ⬛ = Knot stitch to the right (see p. 141)   ⬛ = Ktbl to the right over purl (see p.140)   ⬛ = Ktbl to the left over purl (see p.140)

96 (See photo on p. 56)

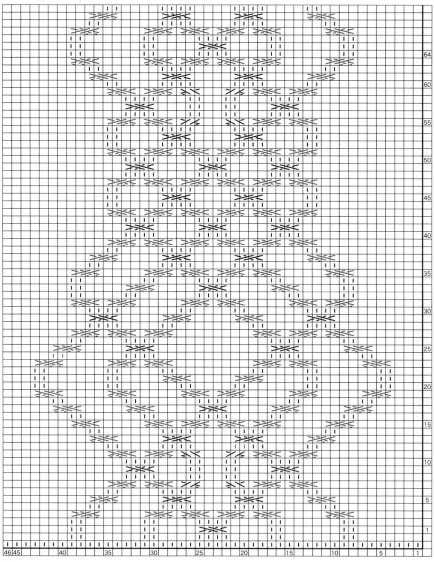

□ = Purl on RS, K on WS

 = Cross 2 to the left over 1 purl (see p. 130)   = Cross 2 to the right over 1 purl (see p. 130)

= Cross 2 to the left over 2 purls (see p. 131)   = Cross 2 to the right over 2 purls (see p. 131)

98 Photo on p.57 (Chart on p. 59)

□ = Purl on RS, K on WS

= Cable 4 to the left (see p. 132)   = Cable 4 to the right (see p. 132)

How to work these symbols
⑬ ⑫ ⑪ ⑩ ⑨ ⑧ ⑦ ⑥ ⑤ ④ ③ ② ①

1) Place st ① on CN, hold to back.
2) Cable 8 to the left with stitches ② through ⑨; knit stitches ⑩ to ⑬.
3) Purl st ① from CN.

⑬ ⑫ ⑪ ⑩ ⑨ ⑧ ⑦ ⑥ ⑤ ④ ③ ② ①

1) Place st ① on CN, hold to back.
2) Knit sts ② to ⑤; cable 8 to the right with sts ⑥ to ⑬.
3) Purl st ① from CN.

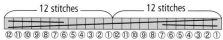

— 12 stitches —   — 12 stitches —
⑫ ⑪ ⑩ ⑨ ⑧ ⑦ ⑥ ⑤ ④ ③ ② ① ⑫ ⑪ ⑩ ⑨ ⑧ ⑦ ⑥ ⑤ ④ ③ ② ①

1) Place sts ① to ⑫ on CN, hold to back.
2) Cable 8 to the left with the next set of sts ① to ⑧; knit sts ⑨ to ⑫.
3) Knit sts ① to ⑫ from CN.

How to work these symbols
⑬ ⑫ ⑪ ⑩ ⑨ ⑧ ⑦ ⑥ ⑤ ④ ③ ② ①

1) Place sts ① to ⑫ on CN, hold to back.
2) Purl st ⑬.
3) Return sts ① to ⑫ to LN; knit sts ① to ④.
4) Cable 8 to the right with sts ⑤ to ⑫.

⑬ ⑫ ⑪ ⑩ ⑨ ⑧ ⑦ ⑥ ⑤ ④ ③ ② ①

1) Place sts ① to ⑫ on CN, hold to front.
2) Purl st ⑬.
3) Return sts ① to ⑫ to LN.
4) Cable 8 to the left with stitches ① to ⑧, then knit sts ⑨ to ⑫.

※Chart explanation on p. 58

102 (See photo on p. 61)

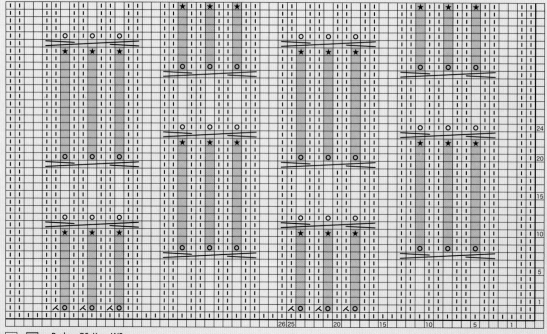

☐ · ▨ = Purl on RS, K on WS

★ = Purl st, then remove needle from the stitch on the next row and let it ladder down; it will stop at the yo below.

See explanation on p. 61

101 Puppy Princess Anny

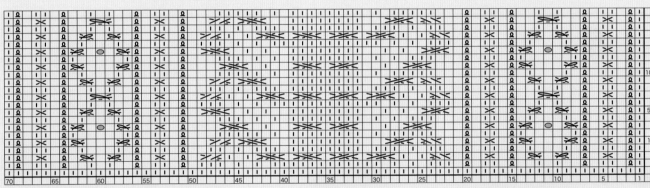

☐ = Purl on RS, K on WS

⬭ = 5 stitch, 3 row bobble (see p. 142)

⧓ = (see p. 130)

⧓ = (see p. 140)

⧓ = (see p. 140)

⧓ = (see p. 130)

⧓ = (see p. 130)

102 pattern, continued

 How to work this symbol

1) Work decreases in row 1 to make 8 stitches (see below).

2) With the same stitches, cable 8 to the right.

☐ = Shaded boxes indicate no stitch
where decreases occurred.

How to work this symbol

1) Cable 8 to the right

☐ = Shaded boxes indicate no stitch.

102 (Chart on p. 60) Diakeito Tasmanian Merino

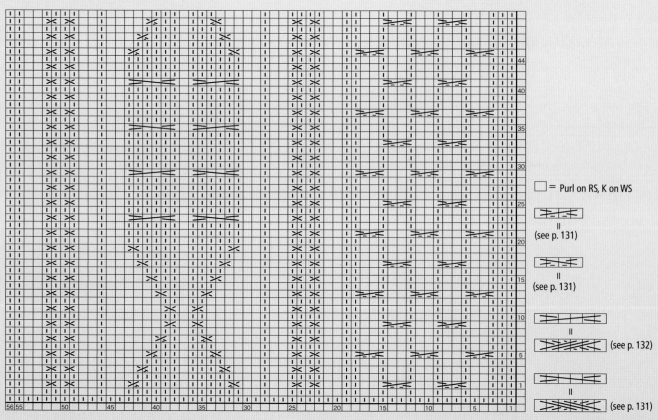

☐ = Purl on RS, K on WS

(see p. 131)

(see p. 131)

(see p. 132)

(see p. 131)

104 Diakeito Tasmanian Merino

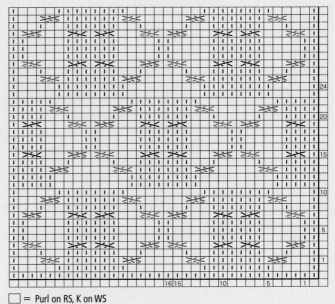

☐ = Purl on RS, K on WS

⊠⊠ = (see p. 131)   ⊠⊠ = (see p. 130)

⊠⊠ = (see p. 131)   ⊠⊠ = (see p. 130)

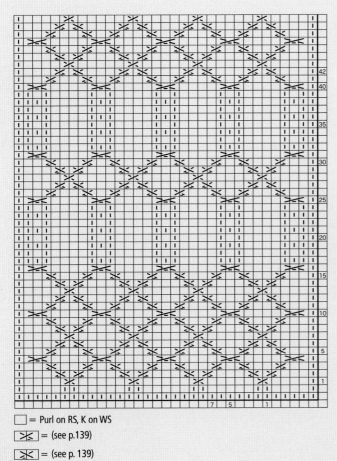

☐ = Purl on RS, K on WS

⊠ = (see p.139)

⊠ = (see p. 139)

⊠⊠ = (see p.131)

105 Hamanaka Organic Wool Mid Fiel

106 (Chart on p. 109) **Puppy Princess Anny**

107 Naito Shoji Zara

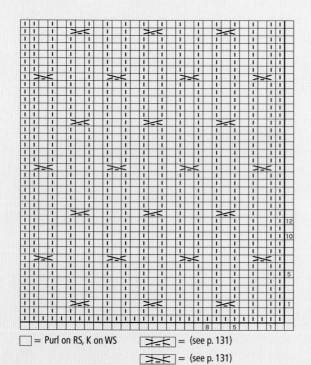

⬜ = Purl on RS, K on WS   ⬛⤬⬛ = (see p. 131)

⬛⤬⬛ = (see p. 131)

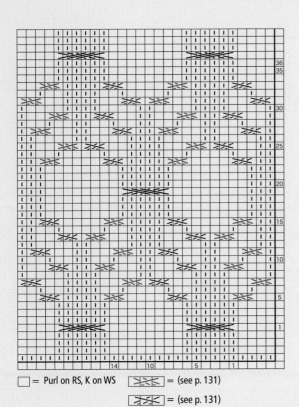

□ = Purl on RS, K on WS 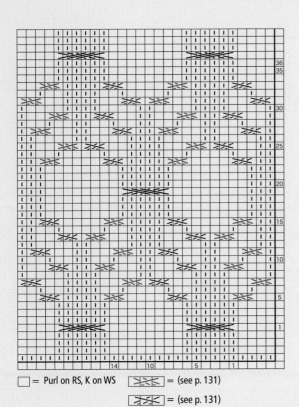 = (see p. 131)

= (see p. 131)

108 Clover Petits Fours

109 (Chart on p. 109) Diakeito Tasmanian Merino

110 Richmore Percent Gradation, Teddy, Soff Spark

(Chart on p. 67)

111-a

111-b

111-a, 111-b Richmore Percent

110 (See photo on p. 66)

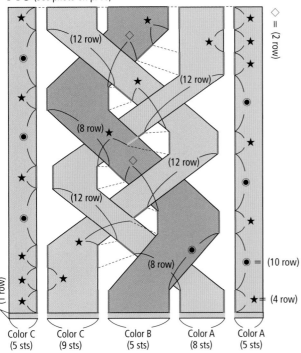

◇ = (2 row)

(12 row)
(12 row)
(8 row)
(12 row)
(12 row)
(8 row)
(1 row)
= (10 row)
★ = (4 row)

Color C (5 sts)　Color C (9 sts)　Color B (5 sts)　Color A (8 sts)　Color A (5 sts)

| = Join the sections as shown by the red lines in illustration above: work across all stitches, changing colors as indicated, for 4 rows each time.

※ Work in stockinette throughout.

111-a, 111b (See photo on p. 66)

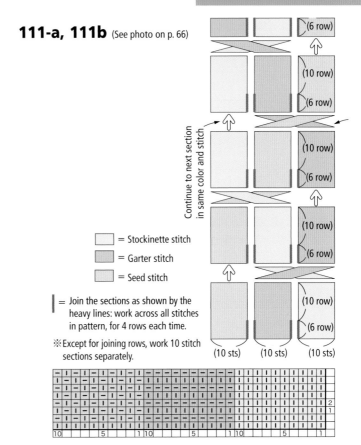

(6 row)
(10 row)
(6 row)
Continue to next section in same color and stitch
(10 row)
(6 row)
(10 row)
(6 row)
(10 row)
(6 row)
(10 sts) (10 sts) (10 sts)

☐ = Stockinette stitch
☐ = Garter stitch
☐ = Seed stitch

| = Join the sections as shown by the heavy lines: work across all stitches in pattern, for 4 rows each time.

※ Except for joining rows, work 10 stitch sections separately.

☐ = Color A　☐ = Color B　☐ = Color C　☐ = Color D
☐ = Color E (3-needle bindoff to outer sections of motifs)

120 (See photo on p.72) Joining motifs

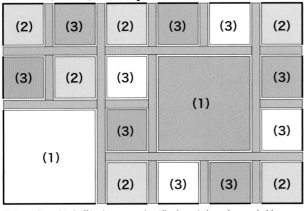

(2) (3) (2) (3) (3) (2)
(3) (2) (3) (3)
(1)
(3) (3)
(1)
(2) (3) (3) (2)

※ Heavy lines: bind off in the same color. All other stitches, place on holders.

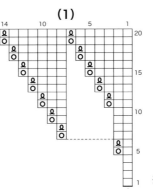

(1)
(2)
(3)

☐ = Knit on RS, P on WS

※ Motifs 1, 2 and 3 are knitted from the center out. See p. 107 for cast-on method.
※ Repeat the charted sections of each motif 4 times around.

61 (See photo on p. 30)

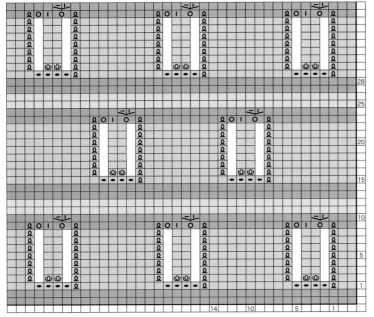

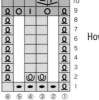

☐ = St st (in each color)
☐ = Color A　☐ = Color B　☐ = Color C

How to work these symbols

1) Work row 1 (RS) as charted: bind off 4 sts..
2) On row 2 (WS), p1tbl, make 2 sts with backward loop (see p. 143), p1tbl.
3) Follow chart for rows 3 to 8.
4) On row 9 (RS), ktbl, yo, then remove LN from stitches ③ and ④ (the next 2 on LN) and let them ladder down.
5) Now insert tip of RN under the lowest laddered strand, front to back, and knit, catching all the loose strands under the stitch.
6) Yo, ktbl.
7) On row 10 (WS), work 2 sts into the second yo as k1, p1.

Three-dimensional Patterns

112 (Chart on p. 110) **Richmore Percent**

113 Hamanaka Etoffe, Span Tear

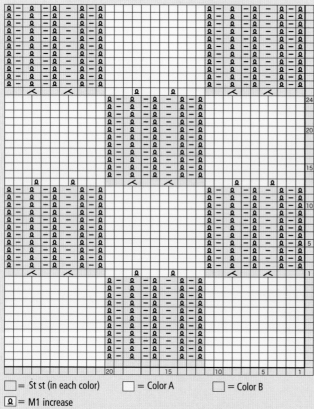

☐ = St st (in each color)   ☐ = Color A   ☐ = Color B

Ω = M1 increase

※When knitting is complete, work 2 decreases in each repeat of color A while
  binding off (as in row 1).

114 Richmore Percent, Suspense

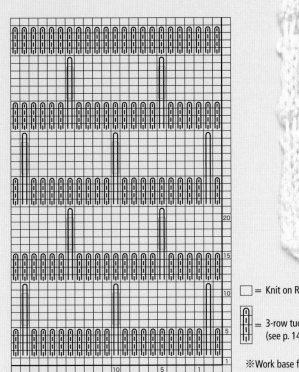

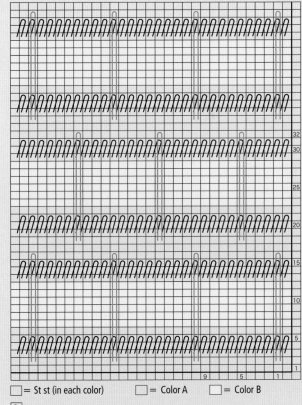

☐ = Knit on RS, P on WS

▯ = 3-row tuck st
(see p. 143)

▯ = 9 row tuck stitch worked on RS

← Wrap the lifted strands 6 times with color B

※Work base fabric in color A

115 Hamanaka Exceed Wool FL Lame, Span Tear

☐ = St st (in each color)   ☐ = Color A   ☐ = Color B

= With RN, lift the purl bump from 2 rows below the second st on LN and k2tog with next st, making a 2-row tuck stitch on the RS (see p. 143).

= With RN, pick up the stitch indicated (14 rows below the next st), pull it up and k2tog with next st (see p. 143).

116 (Explanation on p. 71) Richmore Percent

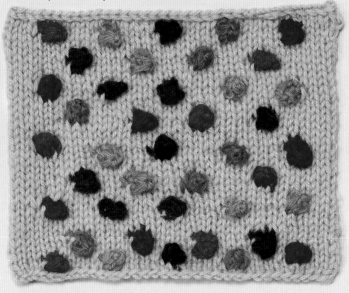

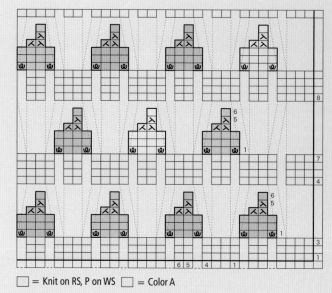

☐ = Knit on RS, P on WS   ☐ = Color A

※Bobbles not worked in color A. (Attach new colors as desired.)
※Bobble see p. 71

117 (Chart on p. 111) Richmore Percent

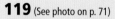

119 (See photo on p. 71)

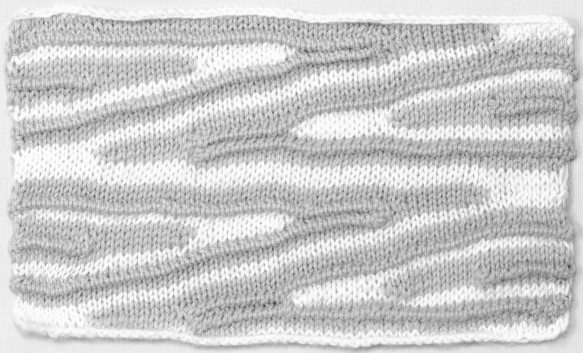

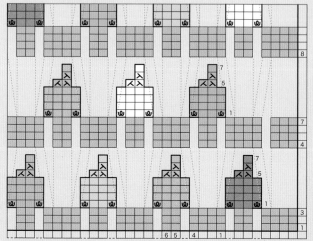

☐ = Knit on RS, P on WS   ☐ = Color A

☐☐ ☐☆☆☐ ☐☐ → ※Bobbles not worked in color A. (Attach new colors as desired.)

How to work this section

④ ③② ①

1) (RS) With color A, k to stitch ③.
2) Turn work. Attach a new color. Work e-wrap increase, p2, e-wrap increase.
3) Follow the chart and work to bobble row 7. Cut yarn; leave st on RN.
4) (RS) Continue with color A and knit 6. Follow the same sequence to make a bobble in another color. Continue across row.
5) Continue knitting with color A. When you reach the stitches indicated by the 2 stars, drop the bobble to the front, and pick up and knit a stitch from each of the e-wrap increases.

※Plan bobbles for color balance
※After completing a bobble, insert the yarn tail in a tapestry needle. From the wrong side, insert the needle into the center of a stitch in the first bobble row, and neaten by sewing the end to the beginning.

116 Continued from p. 70

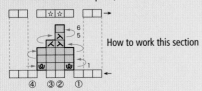

How to work this section

1) With color A, work to stitch ③.
2) Turn work. Attach a new color. Work e-wrap increase, p2, e-wrap increase.
3) Follow the chart and work to bobble row 6. Cut yarn; leave st on RN.
4) (RS) Continue with color A and knit 6. Follow the same sequence to make a bobble in another color. Continue across row.
5) Continue knitting with color A. When you reach the stitches indicated by the star, drop the bobble to the front, and pick up and knit a stitch from each of the e-wrap increases.

※ Plan bobbles for color balance
※ After completing a bobble, insert the yarn tail in a tapestry needle. From the wrong side, insert the needle into the center of a stitch in the first bobble row, and neaten by sewing the end to the beginning.

118 Hamanaka Grand Etoffe and Sonomonono Worsted

119 (Chart on p. 70) Richmore Percent

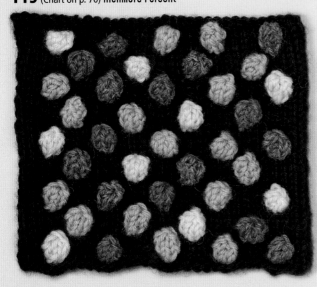

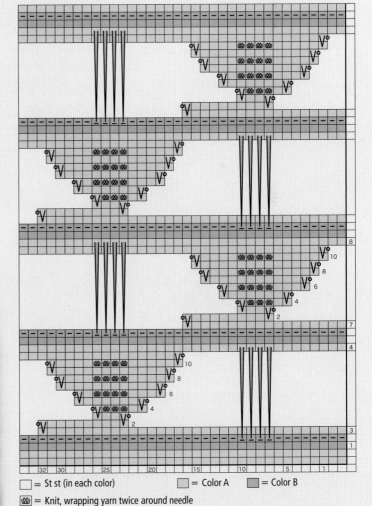

☐ = St st (in each color)   ▨ = Color A   ▩ = Color B

⦿ = Knit, wrapping yarn twice around needle

V = Slip the purl st from row 2

120 (Chart on p. 67) Richmore Percent, Teddy

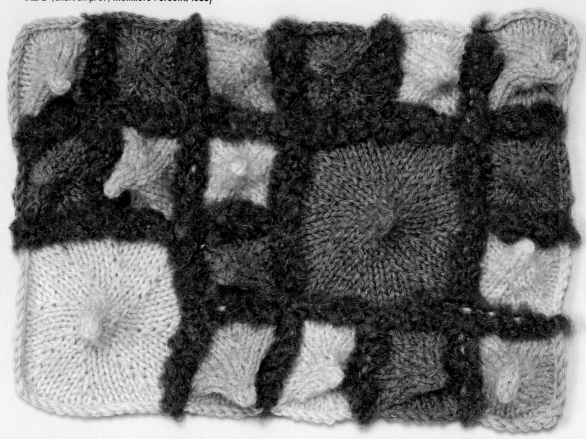

121 (Chart on p. 73) Richmore Percent

121 (See photo on p. 72)

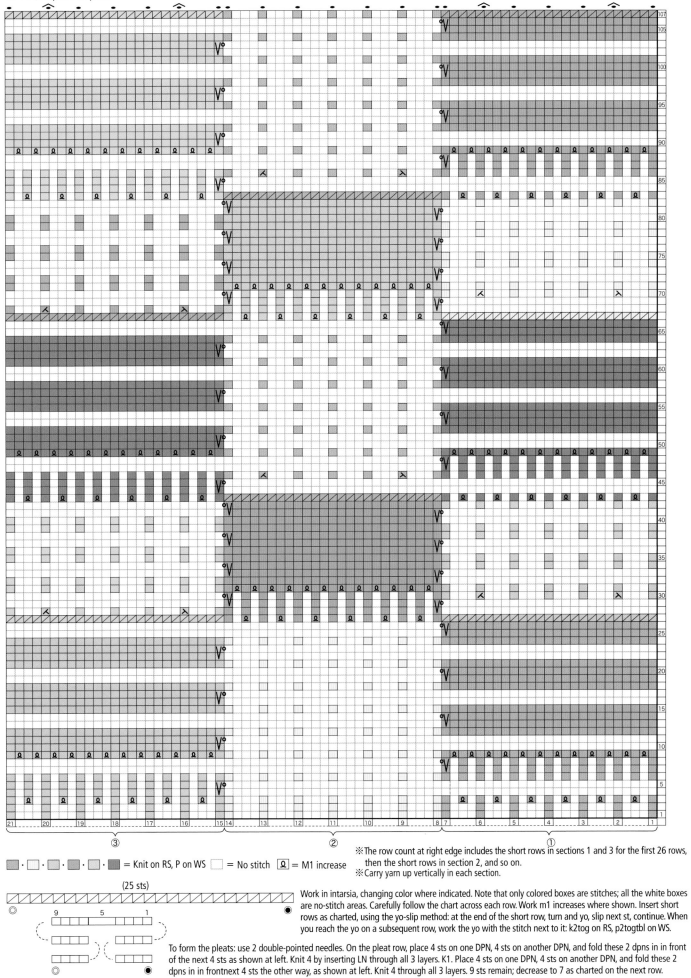

■ · □ · ■ · □ · ■ = Knit on RS, P on WS   □ = No stitch   Ω = M1 increase

(25 sts)

③   ②   ①

※The row count at right edge includes the short rows in sections 1 and 3 for the first 26 rows, then the short rows in section 2, and so on.
※Carry yarn up vertically in each section.

Work in intarsia, changing color where indicated. Note that only colored boxes are stitches; all the white boxes are no-stitch areas. Carefully follow the chart across each row. Work m1 increases where shown. Insert short rows as charted, using the yo-slip method: at the end of the short row, turn and yo, slip next st, continue. When you reach the yo on a subsequent row, work the yo with the stitch next to it: k2tog on RS, p2togtbl on WS.

To form the pleats: use 2 double-pointed needles. On the pleat row, place 4 sts on one DPN, 4 sts on another DPN, and fold these 2 dpns in in front of the next 4 sts as shown at left. Knit 4 by inserting LN through all 3 layers. K1. Place 4 sts on one DPN, 4 sts on another DPN, and fold these 2 dpns in in frontnext 4 sts the other way, as shown at left. Knit 4 through all 3 layers. 9 sts remain; decrease to 7 as charted on the next row.

Lace Motifs

122 Hamanaka Exceed Wool L, Grand Etoffe

Garter stitch
color B

3 row

21 stitches   21 stitches

Lace pattern
color A

21 stitches   21 stitches

Pick up 17 stitches along each edge
Decrease 4 stitches while picking up

21 stitches   21 stitches

※With waste yarn, cast on 126 stitches. The motif consists of 6 sections, repeating stitches 1 to 21.

※When complete, pull the end of the yarn through the remaining 18 stitches and pull tight.

※Remove the waste yarn from the first round, pick up 104 stitches (after the decreases) and work in garter stitch. The decreases are worked by folding the right 4 stitches of the cable section under the left 4 and picking up through 2 stitches at a time.

※When complete, bind off in purl.

8-st cable to the right
(see p. 132)

☐ = Knit on RS, P on WS

Placement of decreases in garter stitch edge

Placement of decreases in garter stitch edge

Lace pattern

3 rows

Edging (use crochet hook)

123 Clover Alpaca Mjuk

☐ = Knit on RS, P on WS

☐ = 3-row brioche stitch (see p. 142)

※With waste yarn, cast on 64 stitches. The motif consists of 4 repeats of stitches 1 to 16.

※When complete, pull the end of the yarn through the remaining 24 stitches and pull tight.

※Remove the waste yarn from the first round. With a crochet hook, work edging as: slip stitch 2 sts together, ch 3 around.

124 (Chart on p. 106) **Hamanaka Exceed Wool FL**

125 Ski Sonata

Circular start with 12 stitches
(see p. 107)

Lace motif

※Cast on with circular start (see p. 107).
  The section of 17 sts is repeated 6 times around.
※Work the last round (102 sts) and bind off in purl.

17 sts = 1 pattern repeat

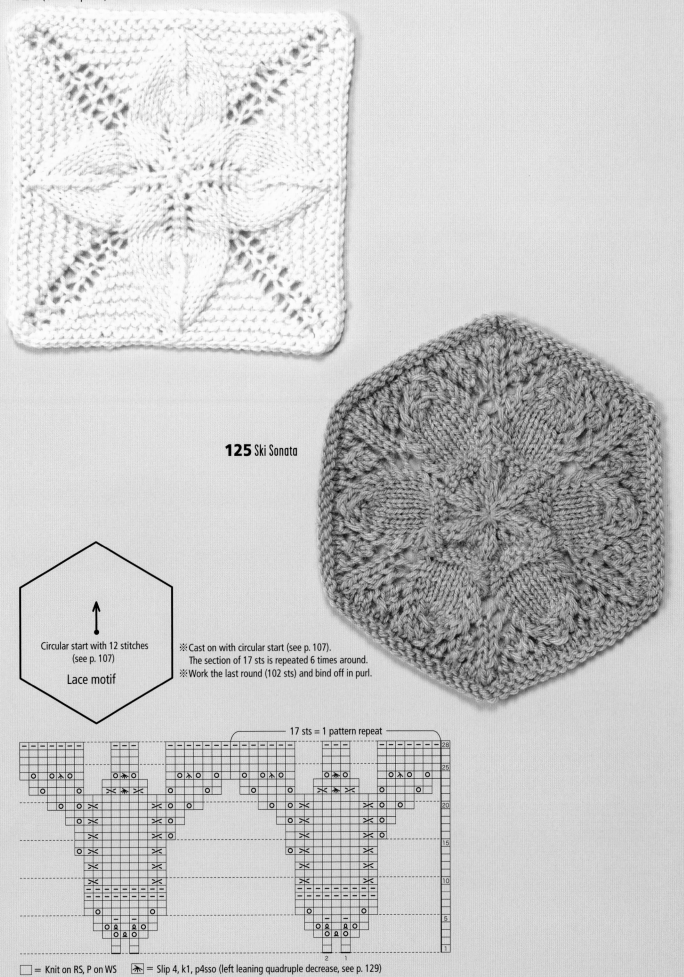

□ = Knit on RS, P on WS   ⚹ = Slip 4, k1, p4sso (left leaning quadruple decrease, see p. 129)

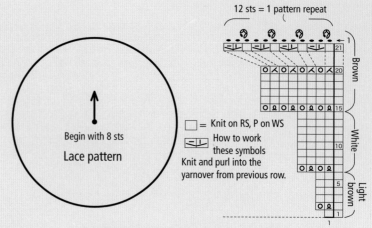

12 sts = 1 pattern repeat

Begin with 8 sts
Lace pattern

☐ = Knit on RS, P on WS

⊏⊐ = How to work these symbols
Knit and purl into the yarnover from previous row.

Brown
White
Light brown

126 Naito Shoji Alpaca Nazka

※Circular cast on (see p. 107) and work 8 pattern repeats around
※Work through round 21 (96 sts)
※After the last knit row, use a crochet hook to bind off in slip st. Insert a 3-st picot every 3rd bind off.

127 Hamanaka Mohair Premier

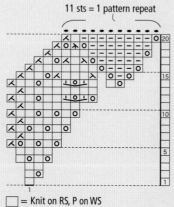

11 sts = 1 pattern repeat

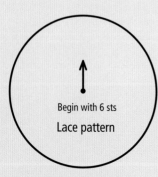

Begin with 6 sts
Lace pattern

※Circular cast on (see p. 100) and work 6 pattern repeats around
※Work through round 20 (66 sts)
※After round 20, bind off in knit.

☐ = Knit on RS, P on WS

⊥|O|⊥ = Make 3 sts by k, yo, k into the same st

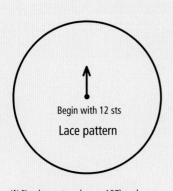

Begin with 12 sts

Lace pattern

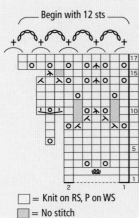

※Circular cast on (see p. 107) and work 6 pattern repeats around
※Work through round 17 (72 sts)
※After round 17, bind off with a crochet hook: sc through 3 sts, ch 5 around.

☐ = Knit on RS, P on WS

▨ = No stitch

◍ = Knit, wrapping yarn twice around needle.

128 Hamanaka Arcoba

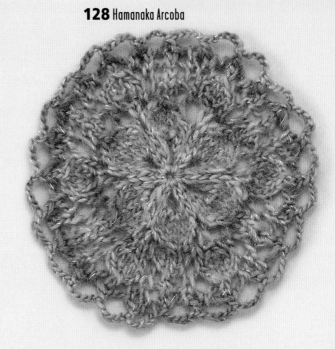

129 (Chart on p. 107 Hamanaka Sonomono Sport

130 Naito Shoji Alpaca Peru

Begin with 8 sts

Lace pattern

※Circular cast on (see p. 107) and work 4 pattern repeats around
※Work through round 19
※After round 19, bind off with a crochet hook: sc through 2 or 3 sts according to the chart, ch 7 around.

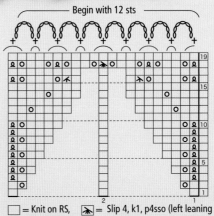

☐ = Knit on RS, P on WS

⟁ = Slip 4, k1, p4sso (left leaning quadruple decrease) (see p. 129)

Edgings

131 (Chart on p. 80) Richmore Percent

132 (Chart on p. 80) Richmore Percent

133 (Chart on p. 80) Diakeito Tasmanian Merino and Puppy Princess Anny

134 (Chart on p. 81) Richmore Percent

135 (Chart on p. 82) Richmore Percent

136 (Chart on p. 81) Richmore Percent

137 (Chart on p. 81) Richmore Percent

138 (Chart on p. 83) Puppy Queen Anny

139 (Chart on p. 83) Richmore Percent

140 (Chart on p. 82) Richmore Percent

131 (Photo on p. 78)

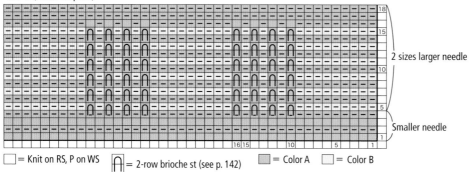

2 sizes larger needle

Smaller needle

☐ = Knit on RS, P on WS ⋒ = 2-row brioche st (see p. 142) ▨ = Color A ☐ = Color B

※ Use waste yarn for a provisional cast-on. When complete, remove the waste yarn and bind off from WS in knit in color A.

※ When complete, bind off in purl from RS in color A.

132 (Photo on p. 78)

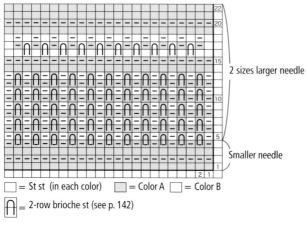

2 sizes larger needle

Smaller needle

☐ = St st (in each color) ▨ = Color A ☐ = Color B

⋒ = 2-row brioche st (see p. 142)

※ Use waste yarn for a provisional cast-on. When complete, remove the waste yarn and bind off from WS in knit.

※ When complete, bind off in purl from RS.

133 (Photo on p. 78)

16 sts = 1 pattern repeat

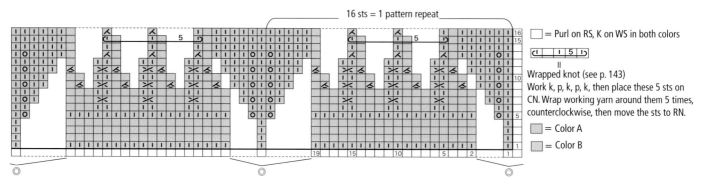

☐ = Purl on RS, K on WS in both colors

⫿ 1 5 ⫾
‖
Wrapped knot (see p. 143)
Work k, p, k, p, k, then place these 5 sts on CN. Wrap working yarn around them 5 times, counterclockwise, then move the sts to RN.

▨ = Color A

▨ = Color B

※ Use waste yarn for a provisional cast-on. When complete, remove the waste yarn and bind off in knit.

※ While binding off after row 16, bind off the sections marked with ◎ with k2tog. Bind off other stitches one at a time.

134 (Photo on p. 78)

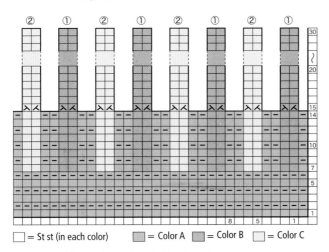

☐ = St st (in each color)　▨ = Color A　▨ = Color B　☐ = Color C

※Cast on with long-tail method. Bind off at the end.
※For rows 7 to 14, carry the contrast color behind the main color.
　For rows 15 to 30, work each color as a separate strip, then tie
　the strips together in pairs (each set of strips ① and ②).

136 (Photo on p. 79)

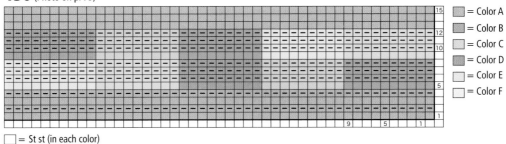

▨ = Color A
▨ = Color B
☐ = Color C
▨ = Color D
☐ = Color E
☐ = Color F

☐ = St st (in each color)

※Cast on with long-tail method. When complete, bind off from WS in purl.
※For rows 5 to 12, carry the contrast yarn vertically from one row to the next.

137 (Photo on p. 79)

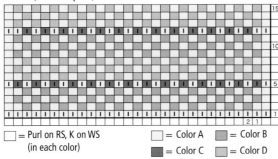

☐ = Purl on RS, K on WS
　(in each color)

☐ = Color A　▨ = Color B
■ = Color C　☐ = Color D

※Cast on with long-tail method.
※Carry yarns up the side edge for color changes.
※When changing colors on rows 5 and 12, keep the contrast color behind RS.
　On all other rows, keep the contrast color in front, and bring it up from below.
※When complete, bind off in knit with color A from WS.

135 (Photo on p. 78)

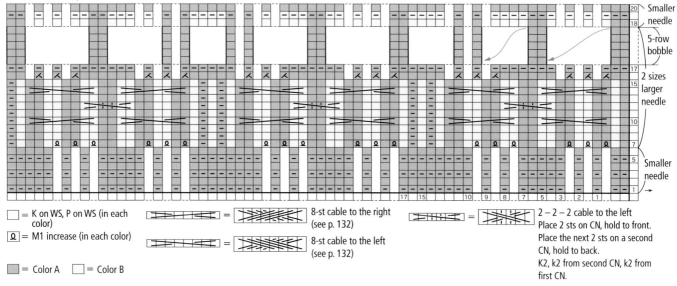

Smaller needle

5-row bobble

2 sizes larger needle

Smaller needle

☐ = K on WS, P on WS (in each color)

Ω = M1 increase (in each color)

 = Color A   ☐ = Color B

[diagram] = [diagram] 8-st cable to the right (see p. 132)

[diagram] = [diagram] 8-st cable to the left (see p. 132)

[diagram] = [diagram] 2 – 2 – 2 cable to the left
Place 2 sts on CN, hold to front. Place the next 2 sts on a second CN, hold to back. K2, k2 from second CN, k2 from first CN.

※Use waste yarn for a provisional cast-on. When complete, remove the waste yarn and bind off from RS in purl.

※For rows 7 to 15 and 18–19, carry the contrast yarn across the back of the work.

※The 5-row bobble (between rows 17 and 18) is a strip of 2 sts. When complete, don't bind off but follow the arrow to the next set of 2 sts.

※When complete, bind off from the RS in purl.

140 (Photo on p. 79)

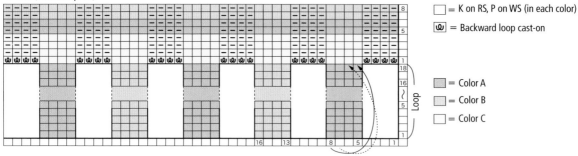

Loop

☐ = K on RS, P on WS (in each color)

ω = Backward loop cast-on

☐ = Color A

☐ = Color B

☐ = Color C

※Each loop consists of 4 sts. Cast on each with waste yarn. After working 18 rows, place on a holder. While working row 1, remove waste yarn for each and knit onto row 1 thus:

※Fold up the cast-on stitches behind the stitches of row 18 as shown by the arrows (keeping RS facing). K2tog each of the sets of sts.

※When complete, bind off in pattern.

139 (Photo on p. 79)

A

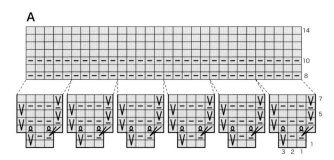

※Cast on each tab separately with long-tail method. When tab is complete (row 7),
   place sts on holder.
※On row 8, pick up and knit sts for each tab from holders.
※After row 14, place all sts on holder.

B

※Cast on each tab separately with long-tail method. When tab is complete (row 7),
   place sts on holder.
※On row 8, pick up and knit sts for each tab from holders.
※On row 11, place the sts from the first section (chart A) behind this section and
   k2tog across, decreasing 1 at left edge.
※After row 14, place all sts on holder.

C

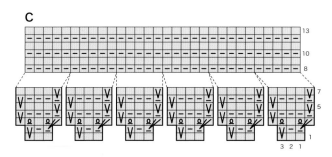

※Cast on each tab separately with long-tail method. When tab is complete (row 7),
   place sts on holder. On row 8, pick up and knit sts for each tab from holders.
※On row 11, place the sts from the second section (chart B) behind this section
   and k2tog across.
※When complete, bind off from the WS in knit.

Reference for 139 charts A to C

☐ = Knit on RS, P on WS   Ω = Ktbl (see p. 136)

Ⅴ = One-row slip st (see p. 142)

How to work this section

1) Knit st in row 2 (WS).
2) On row 3, create st ① by lifting the
   purl bump from row 2 with tip of RN.
3) Then work m1 to create new st ②.

138 (Photo on p. 79)

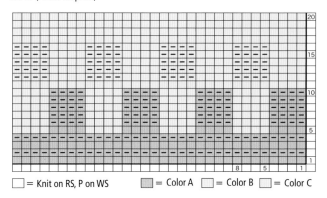

☐ = Knit on RS, P on WS   = Color A   ☐ = Color B   ☐ = Color C

※Cast on with long-tail method. When complete, bind off from RS in knit.
※For rows 5 to 16, carry contrast yarn up the side edge.

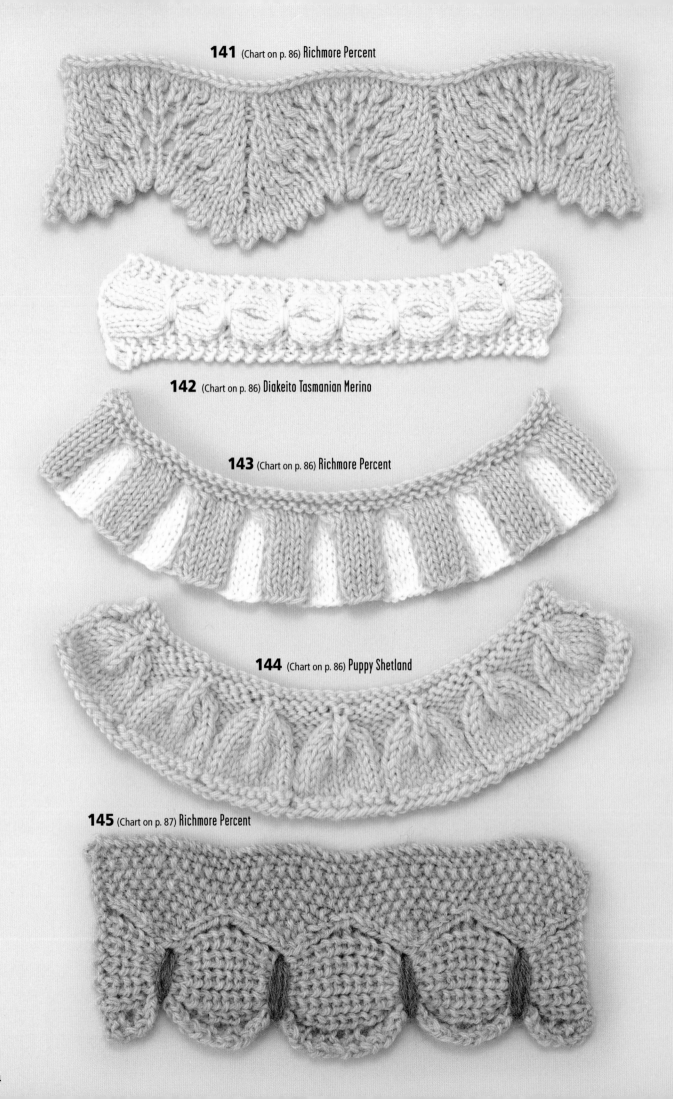

141 (Chart on p. 86) Richmore Percent

142 (Chart on p. 86) Diakeito Tasmanian Merino

143 (Chart on p. 86) Richmore Percent

144 (Chart on p. 86) Puppy Shetland

145 (Chart on p. 87) Richmore Percent

146 (Chart on p. 87) Richmore Percent

147 (Chart on p. 87) Naito Shoji Bio Fine

148 (Chart on p. 87) Puppy New 4Ply

149 (Chart on p. 87) Richmore Percent

150 (Chart on p. 104) Diakeito Tasmanian Merino

141 (Photo on p. 84)

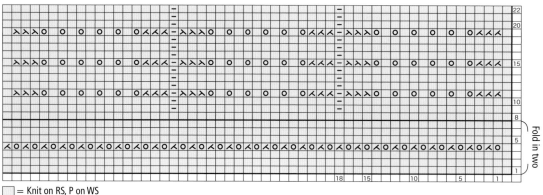

☐ = Knit on RS, P on WS

※Use waste yarn for provisional cast on
※On row 8, fold row 1 to the back. Remove the provisional cast-on and k2tog sts from row 1 with sts from row 8.
※When complete, bind off from RS in knit.

142 (Photo on p. 84)

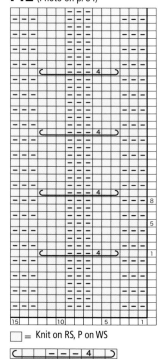

☐ = Knit on RS, P on WS

‖
Wrapped knot (see p. 143)
Work k3, p3, k3, then place these 9 sts on
CN. Wrap working yarn around them 4 times,
counterclockwise, then move the sts to RN.

※Cast on with long-tail method.
※When complete, bind off from WS in purl.

143 (Photo on p. 84)

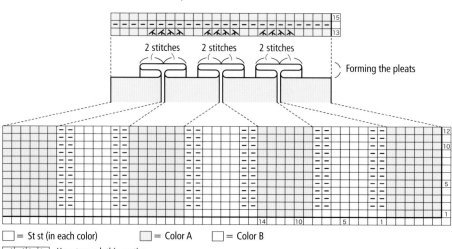

2 stitches 2 stitches 2 stitches → Forming the pleats

☐ = St st (in each color)   ☐ = Color A   ☐ = Color B
⅄⅄⅄⅄ How to work this section
④ ③ ② ①

1) With RS facing, fold the sections of color B behind color A as shown. Work the 3 layers of st ① and ② as slip 1, k2tog, psso.
2) Knit st ② in the same way; one side of pleat done.
3) Work sts ③ and ④ as k3tog through all 3 layers; second part of pleat done.
4) When complete, bind off from RS in knit.

※For rows 1 to 12, carry the contrast color yarn vertically from row to row.
※Cast on for each color section separately with long-tail method.
※When complete, bind off from WS in knit.

144 (Photo on p. 84)

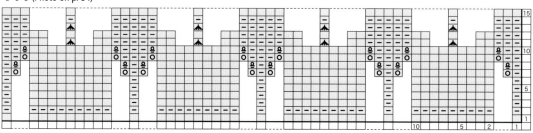

☐ = Knit on RS, P on WS   ⟰ = Centered quadruple decrease (see p. 137)

※Cast on with long-tail method.
※Bind off from WS in knit.

145 (Photo on p. 84)

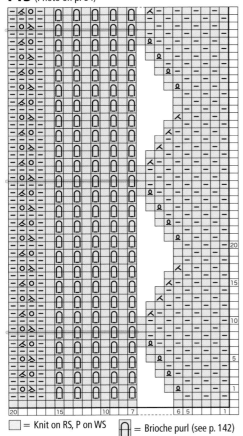

☐ = Knit on RS, P on WS   ⌂ = Brioche purl (see p. 142)

▬▬ = Wrap these 14 sts with color B 5 times, making this section about 2.5 cm (about 1⅓") wide.

※Work the base fabric in color A.
※Cast on with long-tail method.
※When complete, bind off from WS in knit.

146 (Photo on p. 85)

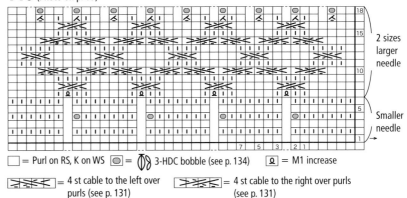

2 sizes larger needle

Smaller needle

☐ = Purl on RS, K on WS   ⊙ = 3-HDC bobble (see p. 134)   Ω = M1 increase

⟩✕✕⟨ = 4 st cable to the left over purls (see p. 131)   ⟩✕✕⟨ = 4 st cable to the right over purls (see p. 131)

※Use a waste yarn to do a provisional cast-on, leaving a length of yarn tail 3 or 4 times the width of the fabric. When complete, remove provisional cast-on and bind off from RS in purl.
※When all rows are complete, bind off from WS in knit.

149 (Photo on p. 85)

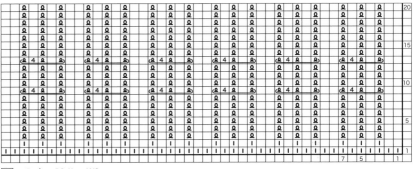

☐ = Purl on RS, K on WS

Ω 4 Ω ⟩⟨ = Wrapped knot (see p. 143). Work ktbl, p, ktbl, p, ktbl, then place these 5 sts on CN. Wrap working yarn around them 4 times, counterclockwise, then move the sts to RN.

※Cast on with long-tail method.
※When complete, bind off in pattern.

147 (Photo on p. 85)

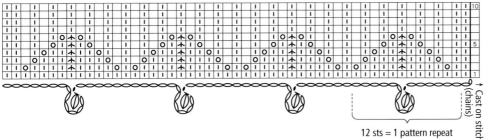

← Cast on stitches (chains)

12 sts = 1 pattern repeat

☐ = Purl on RS, K on WS

 Bobble

1) How to work this edge:
2) Chain 8, then ch 5 to begin bobble
3) Work 3 hdc into 3rd ch from hook. Slip st to the 8th ch.
4) Continue to the next bobble with ch 12.

※Cast on with crochet hook.
※After bobbles are complete, use knitting needle to pick up sts from the back of the chain sts
※When complete, bind off in pattern.

148 (Photo on p. 85)

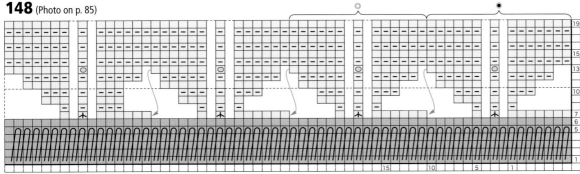

☐ = St st (in each color)
▨ = Color A
☐ = Color B

∐ = 4-row tuck stitch, RS facing (see p. 143)

⊙ = 5-row, 5-stitch knit bobble (see p. 142)

※Use waste yarn for provisional cast-on and work 5 rows in stockinette. On row 6, make tucks by picking up the purl bumps between the next 2 sts behind row 1 and k2tog with the sts of row 6.
※For the parts of rows 7–13 marked with ●, work the triangular section by turning the work. After the 6th turn, follow the arrow and continue to the next section.
※For the parts of rows 7–13 marked with ○, work the triangular section by turning the work. After the 6th turn, follow the arrow and continue to the next section. Repeat across the row.
※Work across all sts for rows 14–19.
※When complete, bind off from WS in knit.

From Pattern to Finished Garment

I've used eleven of the stitch patterns in this book to design a variety of finished items.
I introduce them here, with my designer's comments.
I hope the hints will help you to make the best use of the patterns.

Cardigan with crocheted edging: photo on p. 90

Using pattern 3, with an added crochet edge.

Multicolored fringed cowl: photo on p. 92

Using patterns 87 and 88

Three-dimensional arm warmers: photo on p. 94

Using patterns 120

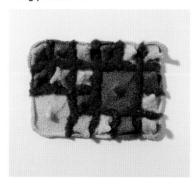 

Fair Isle basket cover: photo on p. 96

Using pattern 67, with an added crochet edge

Fringed mittens: photo on p. 97

Using pattern 75 and 76

White sweater: photo on p. 98

Using pattern 113

Nordic coat: photo on p. 100

Using pattern 72

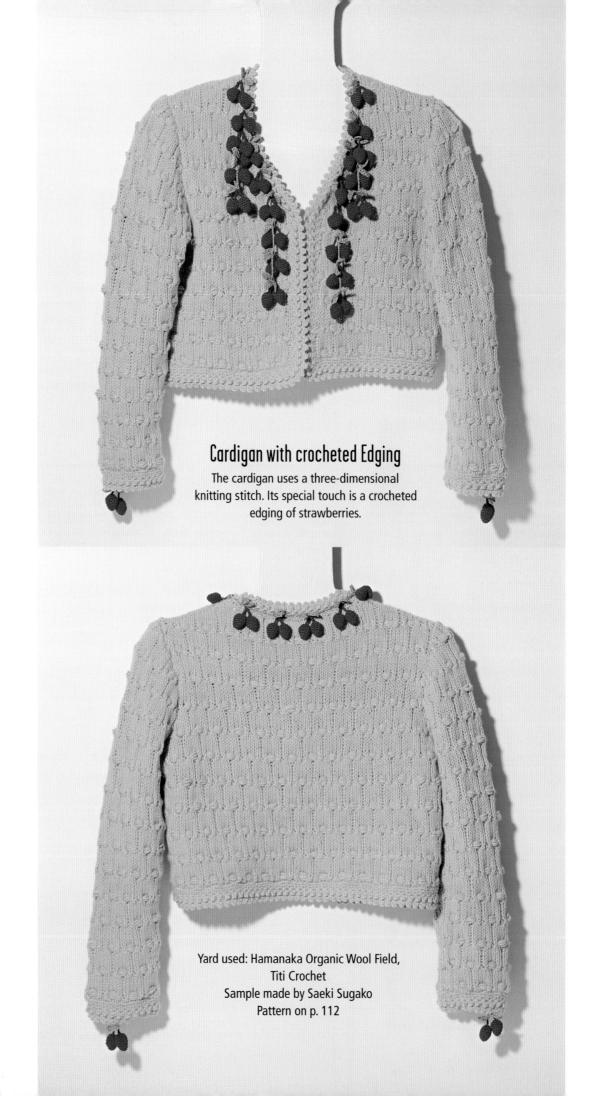

Cardigan with crocheted Edging

The cardigan uses a three-dimensional knitting stitch. Its special touch is a crocheted edging of strawberries.

Yard used: Hamanaka Organic Wool Field,
Titi Crochet
Sample made by Saeki Sugako
Pattern on p. 112

Multicolored fringed cowl

Here is a Fair Isle cowl worked in mostly dark colors. With a fringe
on one edge, it can be worn as a shoulder warmer or a poncho.
Yarn used: Diakeito Dia Tasmanian Merino
Sample made by Yano Akiko
Pattern on p. 115

Three-dimensional arm warmers

Arm warmers made of three motifs joined together,
using natural colors of yarn.
Yarn used: Richmore Percent, Teddy
Sample made by Miyamoto Hiroko
Pattern on p. 117

Fair Isle basket cover

A decorative cover with a Fair Isle pattern to cover
a ready-made basket.
Yarn used: Puppy Princess Anny
Sample made by Nakagawa Yoshiko
Pattern on p. 118

Fringed mittens

Mittens with an Inca-inspired stranded pattern. Fringes are
attached at the wrist. These mittens are thick and warm.
Yarn used: Daruma Prime Merino Worsted
Sample made by Nakagawa Yoshiko
Pattern on p. 119

White sweater

Made with two textures of white yarn, the body of the sweater
has a three-dimensional fabric, while the sleeves are simple.
Yarn used: Hamanaka Etoffe, Span Tear
Sample made by Tsuchitani Miyuki
Pattern on pp. 121

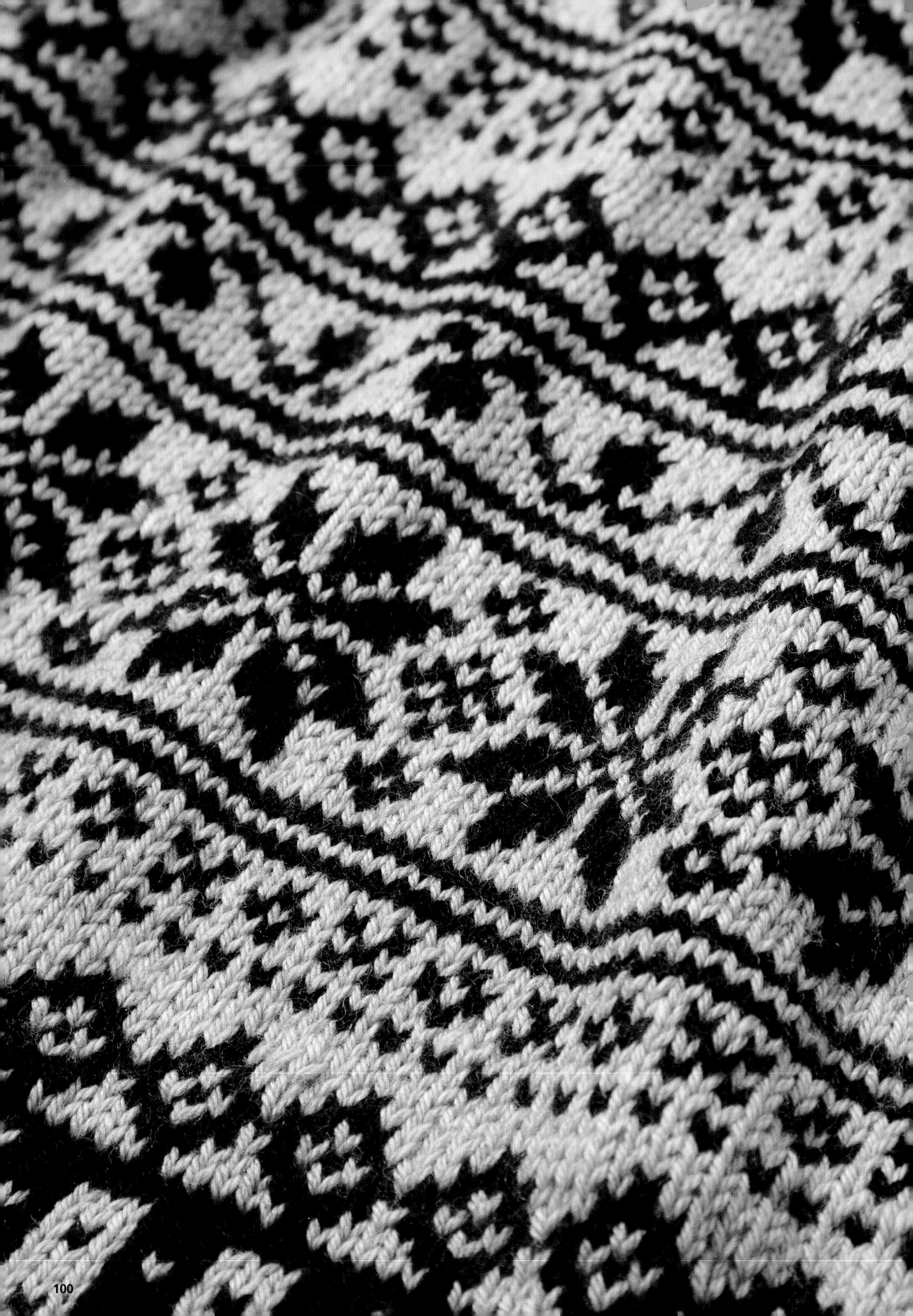

Nordic coat

A coat with Nordic motifs in an easy-to-wear length.
The attached tie adds a cute touch. Yarn used: Ski Menuet

Sample made by Kojima Fumie
Pattern on pp. 124

Yarns Used in These Projects

Yarn name	Used in design(s)	Type (approx.)	Fiber content	Put-up	Ravelry link
Hamanaka Organic Wool Field	Cardigan with crocheted edging	Sport	100% wool	40g = 131 yards (120 meters)	https://www.ravelry.com/yarns/library/hamanaka-organic-wool-field-(discontinued)
Hamanaka Titi Crochet	Cardigan with crocheted edging	Lace	100% cotton	40g = 185 yards(169 meters)	https://www.ravelry.com/yarns/library/hamanaka-titi-crochet-
Diakeito Tasmanian Merino	Multicolor cowl	Sport	100% wool	40g = 131 yards(120 meters)	https://www.ravelry.com/yarns/library/diakeito-tasmanian-merino
Richmore Percent	Three-dimensional arm warmers	DK	100% wool	40g = 131 yards (120 meters)	https://www.ravelry.com/yarns/library/richmore-percent-1-100-
Richmore Teddy	Three-dimensional arm warmers	Bulky	38% Wool, 37% Alpaca, 24% Acrylic, 1% Nylon	30g = 38 yards (35 meters)	https://www.ravelry.com/yarns/library/richmore-teddy_(discontinued)
Puppy Princess Anny	Basket cover	DK	100% wool	40g = 122 yards (112 meters)	https://www.ravelry.com/yarns/library/puppy-princess-anny
Daruma Prime Merino Worsted	Fringed mittens	Worsted	100% wool	40g = 95 yards (86 meters)	NOT IN RAVELRY
Hamanaka Etoffe	White sweater	Aran	70% alpaca, 24% wool, 6% nylon	40g = 110 yards (100 meters)	https://www.ravelry.com/yarns/library/hamanaka-etoffe-(discontinued)
Hamanaka Span Tear	White sweater	Fingering	68% Polyester, 13% Mohair, 10% Nylon, 9% Wool	25g = 137 yards (125 meters)	https://www.ravelry.com/yarns/library/hamanaka-span-tear
Ski Menuet	Nordic coat	Worsted	100% wool	40g = 94 yards (86 meters)	https://www.ravelry.com/yarns/library/ski-yarn-menuet

How to Make

Stitch diagrams and instructions for
the following patterns can also be
found in these pages:

A table of the symbols used in the patterns in this book
can be found on pages 128–135.

17

(Photo on p. 13)

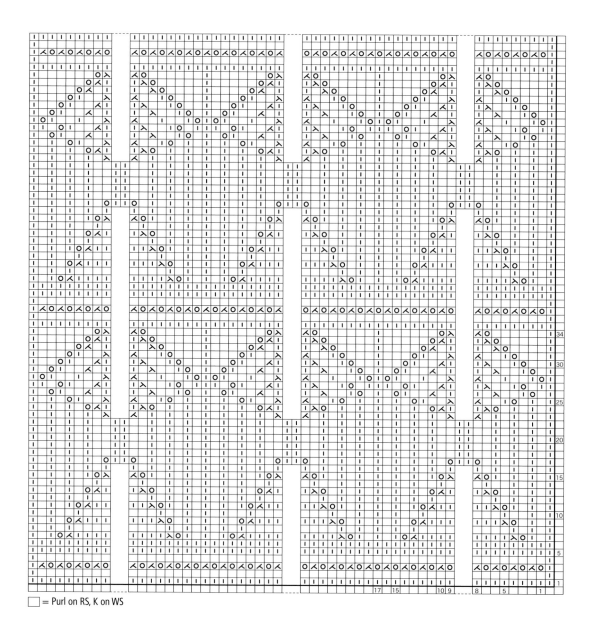

☐ = Purl on RS, K on WS

150

(Photo on p. 85)

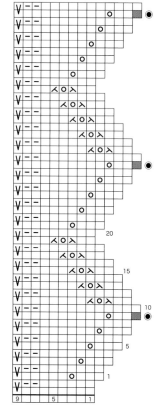

☐ = Knit on RS, P on WS

V̶ = Slip stitch (see p.142)

⊙ How to work the triple leaf

⬛ = Triple leaf

7 rows = one repeat

☐†☐○☐†☐ = Knit, yarnover, knit into this stitch

1) On row 1, make 3 sts into the st marked with ⬛. Work these 3 sts for 7 rows, ending with CDD.
2) On row 8, work 3 sts (k, yo, k) into the centered double decrease and the original stitch marked with ⬛, held together. Work these 3 sts for 7 rows.
3) On row 15, with tip of LN, pick up the purl bump behind the last st of the first repeat, then work (k, yo, k) into this st and the CDD together. Work these 3 sts for 7 rows.
4) At the row marked with ★ (following row 21), k2tog the last st of CDD with the last st of the second repeat.
5) Continue with next st on LN.

※Use the long-tail cast-on method.
※When knitting is complete, bind off from RS in knit.

41 (Photo on p. 22)

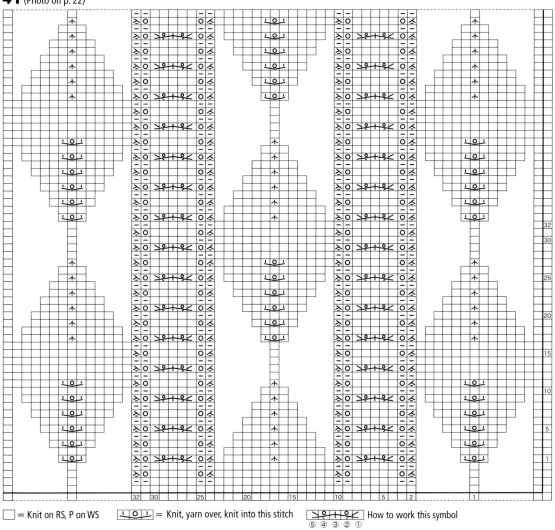

☐ = Knit on RS, P on WS ⊥○⊥ = Knit, yarn over, knit into this stitch How to work this symbol ⑤ ④ ③ ② ①

1) With yarn in back go behind st ① and knit st ②.
2) Move st ② to RN, letting st ① drop to the front. Pick up st ① with tip of LN.
3) Yo. Slip sts ① and ③ to RN as if to k2tog, without working them.
4) Go in front of st ④ and k st ⑤. Pass slipped sts ③ and ① over st ⑤.
5) Yo, k st ④, let st ⑤ drop off LN.

124 (Photo on p. 75)

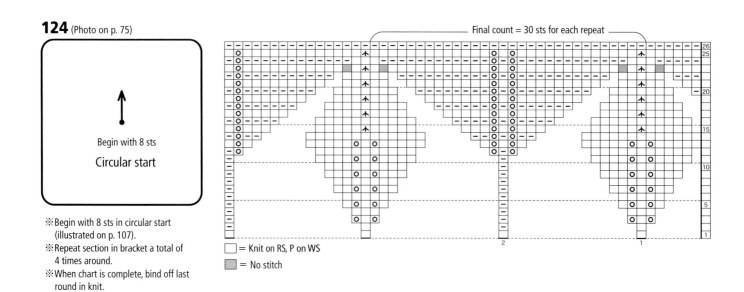

Final count = 30 sts for each repeat

Begin with 8 sts

Circular start

※Begin with 8 sts in circular start (illustrated on p. 107).
※Repeat section in bracket a total of 4 times around.
※When chart is complete, bind off last round in knit.

☐ = Knit on RS, P on WS

▨ = No stitch

92 (Photo on p. 54)

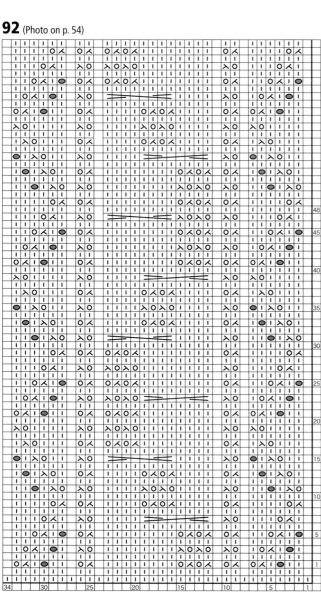

☐ = Purl on RS, K on WS

◉ = 2-HDC bobble (see p. 134)

= 8-st cable to the right (see p. 132)

= 8-sts cable to the left (see p. 132)

Circular start for lace motifs

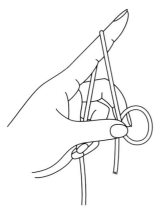

❶ With yarn over index finger, form the yarn into the shape of the numeral 6 to form a loop.

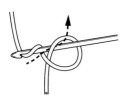

❷ Insert the hook into the loop and yarn over. Pull loop through.

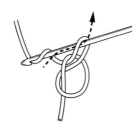

❸ Yarn over hook again, and pull out another loop. One stitch cast on.

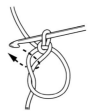

❹ Leaving the first st on hook, insert the hook into the original loop again, under both strands, as shown by the arrow. Yarn over and pull loop through.

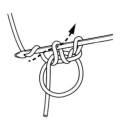

❺ Yarn over and pull out another loop. Second stitch cast on.

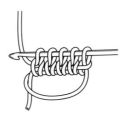

❻ Repeat steps ④ and ⑤ until you have cast on the number of stitches required.

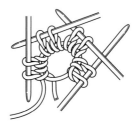

❼ Transfer the cast-on stitches to 3 or 4 double-pointed needles, as needed. These cast-on stitches form row 1 of the stitch pattern.

129 (Photo on p. 77)

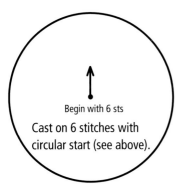

Begin with 6 sts

Cast on 6 stitches with circular start (see above).

※ Repeat section in bracket a total of 3 times around.
※ Row 19 final count: 60 stitches
※ Work the last round with a crochet hook. Cluster 2 or 3 sts (as indicated) and work sc, chain 7 around to form loops.

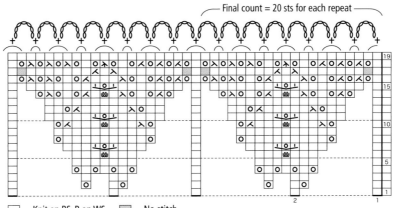

Final count = 20 sts for each repeat

☐ = Knit on RS, P on WS   ▨ = No stitch

⟨QQ⟩ = Knit, wrapping yarn twice around needle.   ⟨I O I⟩ = Knit, yarn over, knit into this stitch (see p. 138).

100

(Photo on p.60)

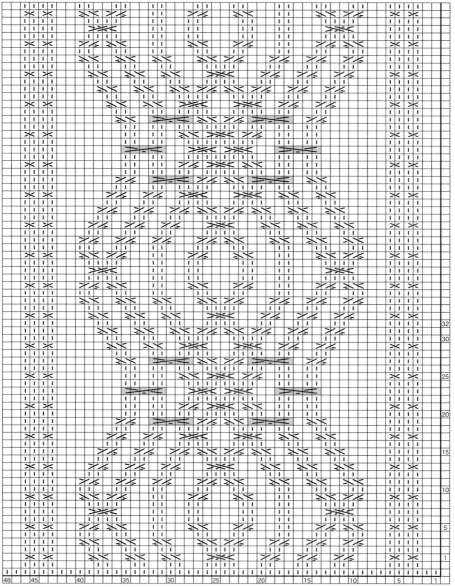

= Purl on RS, K on WS

2-over-3 cable to the left with center purl (see p. 140)

2-over-3 cable to the right with center purl (see p. 140)

109

(Photo on p.65)

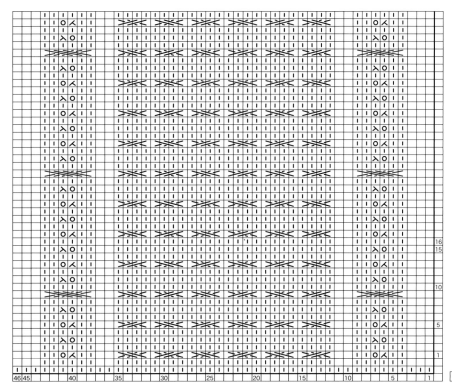

□ = Purl on RS, K on WS

106

(Photo on p. 64)

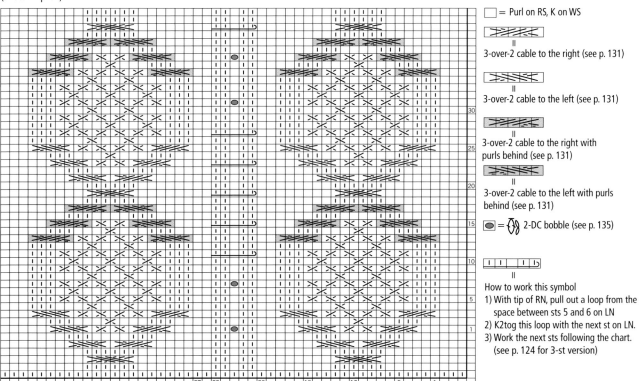

□ = Purl on RS, K on WS

‖
3-over-2 cable to the right (see p. 131)

‖
3-over-2 cable to the left (see p. 131)

‖
3-over-2 cable to the right with
purls behind (see p. 131)

‖
3-over-2 cable to the left with purls
behind (see p. 131)

◉ = 2-DC bobble (see p. 135)

‖
How to work this symbol
1) With tip of RN, pull out a loop from the
space between sts 5 and 6 on LN
2) K2tog this loop with the next st on LN.
3) Work the next sts following the chart.
(see p. 124 for 3-st version)

112 (Photo on p. 68)

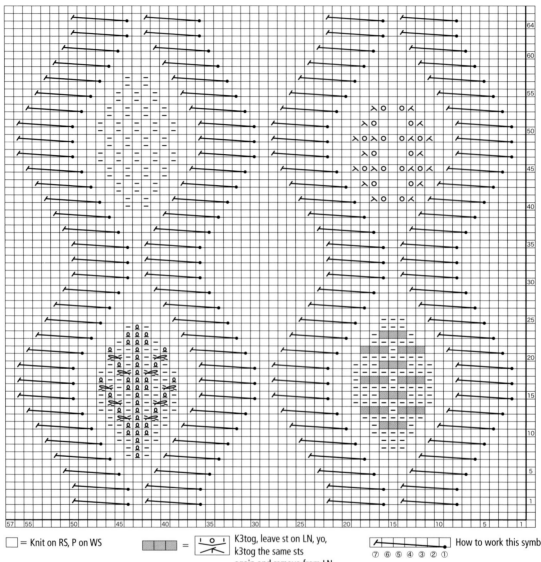

☐ = Knit on RS, P on WS

⬚⬚⬚ = │ᴏ│ / = K3tog, leave st on LN, yo,
⮾ k3tog the same sts
again and remove from LN

⧓ = Cross 1 ktbl to the left
over purl (see p. 140)

⧓ = Cross 1 ktbl to the right
over purl (see p. 140)

⌐────────┐ How to work this symbol
⑦ ⑥ ⑤ ④ ③ ② ①

1) Knit sts ① to ⑥.
2) With tip of LN, pick up the purl loop from below st ①.
Place it on LN and k2tog with st ⑦.

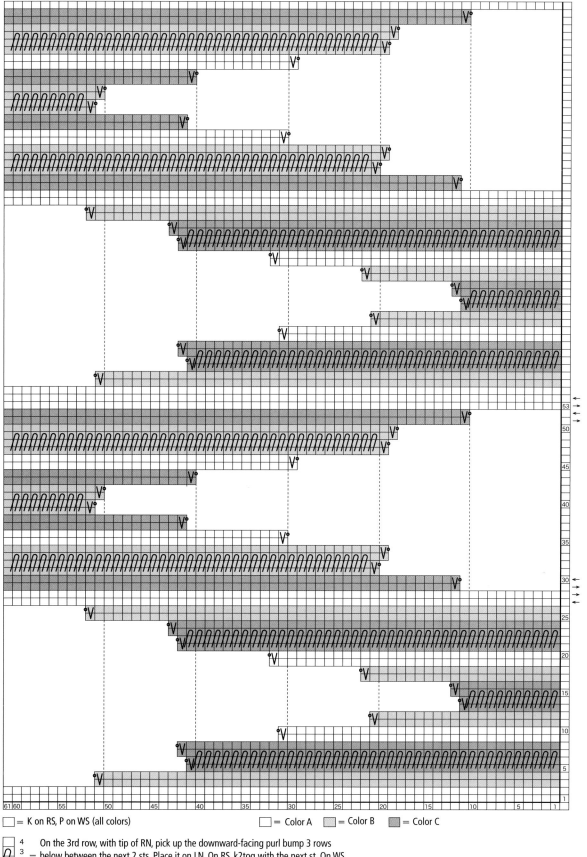

□ = K on RS, P on WS (all colors) □ = Color A □ = Color B ■ = Color C

4
3 On the 3rd row, with tip of RN, pick up the downward-facing purl bump 3 rows
2 = below between the next 2 sts. Place it on LN. On RS, k2tog with the next st. On WS,
1 p2togtbl with the next st. (See p. 143 for 6-row version of this stitch.)

How to work this chart:
1) Work the first 6 rows in stockinette, with short rows as indicated. For each short row, turn, yo, slip first st.
2) On row 7, pick up the purl bumps to make tucked row as described above.
3) Continue as charted, changing colors at right edge. When you come to the yo of a short row, work it with the next stitch: k2tog on RS, p2togtbl on WS.
4) On row 29, slide all sts to the other end of a circular needle (or transfer to another needle—see arrows at right of chart) For the next repeat, work from WS, changing colors at the left edge and continuing to follow chart.
5) Repeat from row 1.

Cardigan with crocheted edging P90

Yarns used for cardigan, Hamanaka Organic Wool Field, beige (color 2), 290g

Substitution Sport weight 100% wool, approximately 1050 yards (950 meters)

For appliques Hamanaka Titi Crochet: red (color 9), 55g, and green (color 24), 10g.

Substitution Lace weight cotton crochet thread, approximately 270 yards (250 meters) in red and 50 yards (48 meters) in green.

Needles US size 6 (3.9mm, Japanese size 6) and crochet hooks in US sizes B and D (2.3mm and 3.0mm, Japanese sizes 3/0 and 5/0) or size to obtain gauge

Finished measurements Bust circumference 38¼ in (97 cm); across shoulders 14¼ in (36 cm); cardigan length 16⅜ in (41.5 cm); sleeve length 20⅜ in (52.5 cm).

Gauge In stitch pattern, 21 stitches and 24 rows = 4 in (10 cm)

INSTRUCTIONS

Use the long-tail cast-on for body and sleeves. Knit those pieces in stitch pattern. Join the shoulders with 3-needle bind-off, then sew the side and underarm seams (but don't attach sleeves at this point). Finish the stitch pattern on body and sleeves by cutting 8 strands of yarn for each woven pattern row, and weaving them through the yarnovers. Using the US size D (3.0mm, Japanese size 5/0) crochet hook, work the crocheted edging around the hem, front bands, collar and sleeve edges. Sew the sleeves into the armscyes. Make the strawberry appliques and sew them onto the cardigan at the places shown in the illustration (p. 114).

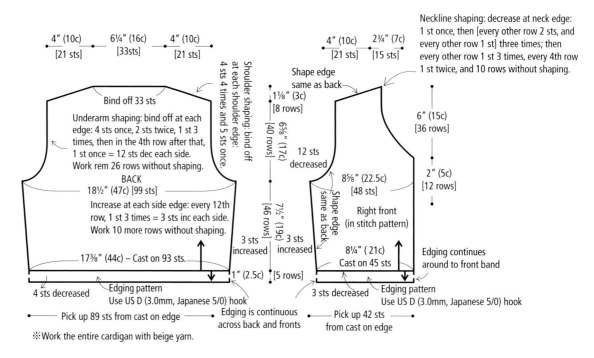

Neckline shaping: decrease at neck edge: 1 st once, then [every other row 2 sts, and every other row 1 st] three times; then every other row 1 st 3 times, every 4th row 1 st twice, and 10 rows without shaping.

4" (10c) [21 sts]   6¼" (16c) [33sts]   4" (10c) [21 sts]

Shoulder shaping: bind off at each shoulder edge: 4 sts 4 times and 5 sts once.

Bind off 33 sts

Underarm shaping: bind off at each edge: 4 sts once, 2 sts twice, 1 st 3 times, then in the 4th row after that, 1 st once = 12 sts dec each side. Work rem 26 rows without shaping.

BACK
18½" (47c) [99 sts]

Increase at each side edge: every 12th row, 1 st 3 times = 3 sts inc each side. Work 10 more rows without shaping.

17⅜" (44c) – Cast on 93 sts.

1" (2.5c) [5 rows]

4 sts decreased   Edging pattern Use US D (3.0mm, Japanese 5/0) hook

Pick up 89 sts from cast on edge   Edging is continuous across back and fronts

※Work the entire cardigan with beige yarn.

4" (10c) [21 sts]   2¾" (7c) [15 sts]

Shape edge same as back

1⅛" (3c) [8 rows]

6⅝" (17c) [40 rows]

6" (15c) [36 rows]

12 sts decreased

7½" (19c) [46 rows]

8⅝" (22.5c) [48 sts]

Shape edge same as back

2" (5c) [12 rows]

Right front (in stitch pattern)

3 sts increased   3 sts increased

8¼" (21c) Cast on 45 sts

Edging continues around to front band

Edging pattern Use US D (3.0mm, Japanese 5/0) hook

3 sts decreased

Pick up 42 sts from cast on edge

Sleeve cap shaping: bind off at each side edge: 2 sts once, then 2 sts 4 times, 1 st 8 times, 2 sts 4 times, and 2 rows without shaping = 26 sts dec each side.

Bind off rem 19 sts

26 sts decreased

5½" (14c) [34 rows]

13" (33c) [73 sts]

Sleeve (in stitch pattern) US size 6 (3.9mm, Japanese size 6) needle

14¼" (36c) [86 rows]

11 sts increased

Underarm shaping: every 10th row, inc 1 st at each edge 5 times; then every 6th row, inc 1 st at each edge 4 times; then every 4th row, inc 1 st each edge twice = 11 sts increased on each side. Work 4 more rows without shaping.

9" (23c) [49 sts] Cast on 49 sts

1" (2.5c) [5 rows]

5 sts decreased   Edging pattern Use US D (3.0mm, Japanese 5/0) hook

Pick up 44 sts from cast on edge

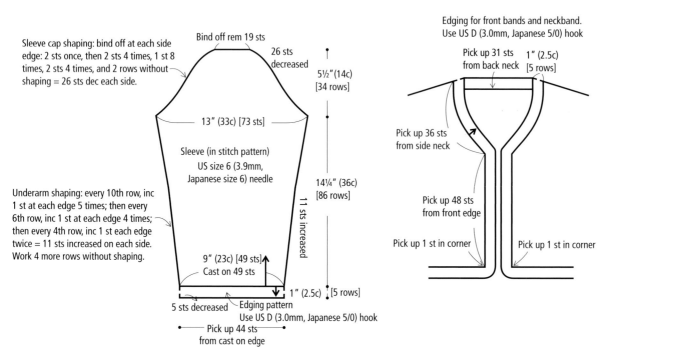

Edging for front bands and neckband. Use US D (3.0mm, Japanese 5/0) hook

Pick up 31 sts from back neck   1" (2.5c) [5 rows]

Pick up 36 sts from side neck

Pick up 48 sts from front edge

Pick up 1 st in corner   Pick up 1 st in corner

Stitch pattern

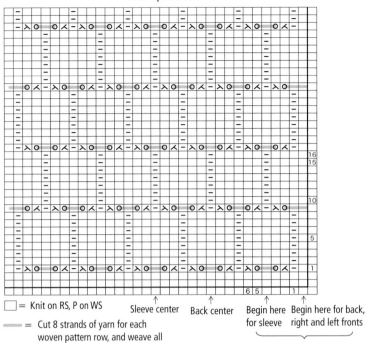

| = Knit on RS, P on WS

Sleeve center · Back center · Begin here for sleeve · Begin here for back, right and left fronts

$\sim$ = Cut 8 strands of yarn for each woven pattern row, and weave all strands through the yarnovers.

Edging pattern. Use US D (3.0mm, Japanese 5/0) hook

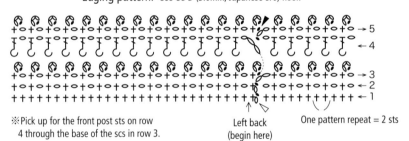

※Pick up for the front post sts on row 4 through the base of the scs in row 3.

Left back (begin here)

One pattern repeat = 2 sts

Turning corner in edging pattern

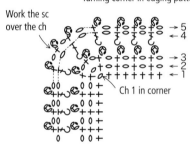

Work the sc over the ch

Ch 1 in corner

Strawberry. Use 3/0 hook

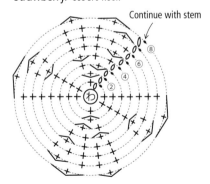

Continue with stem

わ = circular start. (Similar to p. 107, but work scs into loop.)

※Bring yarn tail to the center, then run yarn through the sts in round 8 and pull together at top.

Long strawberry strand. Use US D (3.0mm, Japanese 5/0) hook 3/0 hook and 1 strand of yarn. Make 1.

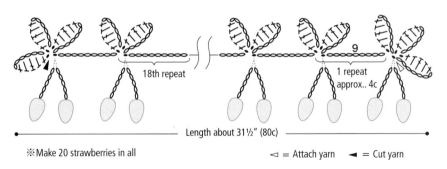

18th repeat

1 repeat approx.. 4c

Length about 31½" (80c)

※Make 20 strawberries in all

◁ = Attach yarn ◀ = Cut yarn

Strawberry (stem and leaf).
Use US B (2.3mm, Japanese 3/0) hook

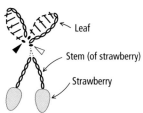

- Leaf
- Stem (of strawberry)
- Strawberry

Colors used	
Strawberry	Red
Stem	Red
Leaf	Green

※After finishing a strawberry, chain 5 to make the stem
※Attach stem to leaves: slip st the start of leaf to the
  5th chain of the stem as shown.

Short strawberry strand with US B (2.3mm, Japanese 3/0) hook; make 2

◁ = Attach yarn
◀ = Cut yarn

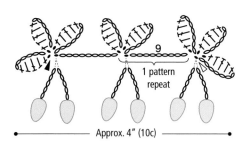

9

1 pattern
repeat

●————— Approx. 4" (10c) —————●

Placement of the strawberry appliques:
sew on as shown

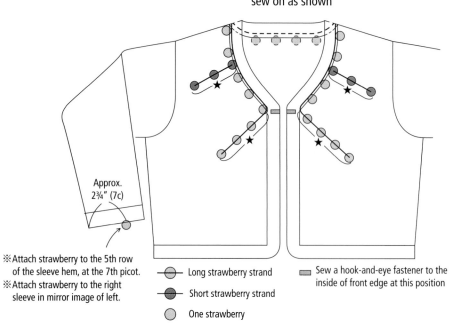

Approx.
2¾" (7c)

※Attach strawberry to the 5th row
  of the sleeve hem, at the 7th picot.
※Attach strawberry to the right
  sleeve in mirror image of left.

◯— Long strawberry strand

●— Short strawberry strand

◯ One strawberry

▭ Sew a hook-and-eye fastener to the
  inside of front edge at this position

※Sew on appliques at the halfway point of each chain linking the pairs of strawberries
※Where marked with ★, don't sew on; let these sections hang freely

Multicolored fringed cowl P93

Yarn used Diakeito Tasmanian Merino, colors:
Light pink (color 736), 25g
Yellow-brown (color 712), 10g
Red (color 717), 25g
Black (color 730), 70g
Natural (color 702), 10g
Lavender (color 722), 15g
Blue (color 740), 20g
Blue-green (color 711), 10g
Substitution Use sport-weight 100% wool. Yardages:
Light pink, 90 yards (82 meters)
Yellow-brown, 35 yards (32 meters)
Red, 90 yards (82 meters)
Black, 235 yards (220 meters)
Natural, 35 yards (32 meters)

Lavender, 50 yards (45 meters)
Blue, 70 yards (65 meters)
Blue-green, 35 yards (32 meters)
Needles US size 6 (3.9mm, Japanese size 6), double-pointed or circular US size 3 (3.3mm, Japanese size 4) or size to obtain gauge
Finished size Depth 11⅞ in (30 cm) (including fringe)
Circumference 45¼ in (115 cm)
Gauge in stranded pattern 23 stitches and 29 rows to 4 in (10 cm)

INSTRUCTIONS

Use waste yarn for a provisional cast-on. Continue in stranded pattern as charted. When main chart is complete, remove the provisional cast-on and work the 13 rows of stripe pattern. Use straight stitch to embroider the "X" shapes. Add fringe to the other edge, following the illustration.

※Attach fringes in 33 places

(8 sts between fringes)

Cowl (Stranded pattern)

Provisional cast on 264 sts: 45¼" (115c)

Striped pattern

2⅜" (6c)

7¾" (19.5c) [57 rows]

1¾" (4.5c) [13 rows]

Total 264 sts: 45¼" (115c)

※Use US size 6 (3.9mm, Japanese size 6) needle unless otherwise noted

Stripe pattern Repeat = 8 sts x 13 rows

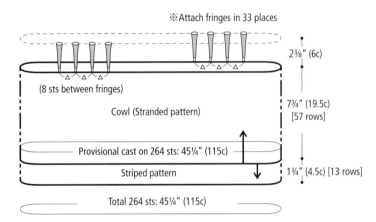

Bind off in purl
Color A
Color 4 with US needle size 3 (3.3mm, Japanese size 4)
Color G
Color A

☐ = Knit

※Secure the embroidery strands by passing them behind these stitches (33 repeats around)

Use one strand each of colors B, C and D together, and embroider the "X" shapes in straight stitch.

Stranded pattern and fringe attachment method

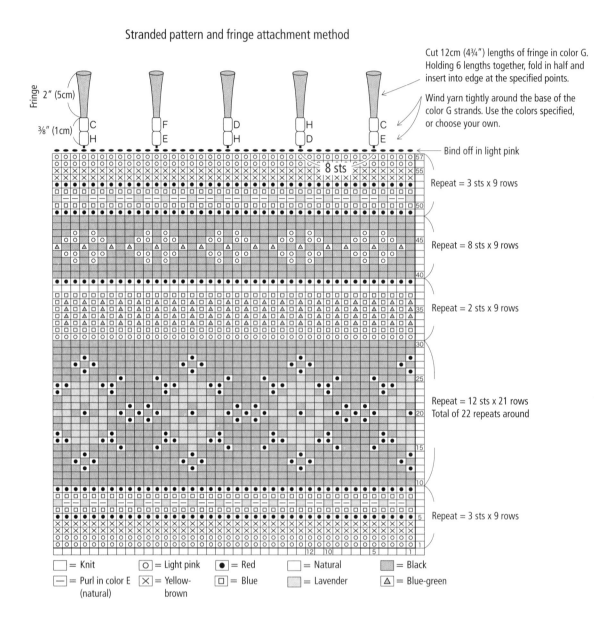

Cut 12cm (4¾") lengths of fringe in color G. Holding 6 lengths together, fold in half and insert into edge at the specified points.

Wind yarn tightly around the base of the color G strands. Use the colors specified, or choose your own.

Fringe 2" (5cm)

⅜" (1cm)

C H | F E | D H | H D | C E

Bind off in light pink

8 sts

Repeat = 3 sts x 9 rows

Repeat = 8 sts x 9 rows

Repeat = 2 sts x 9 rows

Repeat = 12 sts x 21 rows
Total of 22 repeats around

Repeat = 3 sts x 9 rows

| | = Knit | ○ | = Light pink | ● | = Red | | = Natural | | = Black |
| — | = Purl in color E (natural) | ✕ | = Yellow-brown | □ | = Blue | | = Lavender | △ | = Blue-green |

116

Three-dimensional arm warmers P94

Yarn used Richmore Percent, colors:
Gray (color 97), 10g
Brown (color 100), 15g
Light brown (color 98), 20g
Light beige (color 120), 15g
Richmore Teddy brown (color 7), 30g
Substitution Motifs Use DK-weight 100% wool in colors:
Gray, 35 yards (32 meters)
Brown, 50 yards (45 meters)
Light brown, 70 yards (64 meters)
Light beige, 50 yards (45 meters)
Use bulky-weight wool blend boucle yarn in brown, 40 yards (35 meters)
Needles Double-pointed needles US size 9 (5.7mm, Japanese size 12), double-pointed needles US size 4 (3.6mm, Japanese size 5), crochet hook US size D (3.0mm, Japanese size 5/0) or size to obtain gauge

Finished measurements around arm 7½ in (19 cm), length 12⅝ in (32 cm)
Gauge in garter stitch (with boucle), 12.5 stitches and 18 rows. See schematic for measurement of each motif.

INSTRUCTIONS
Knit each motif, and leave stitches live after the last row. Arrange the completed motifs as shown in the schematic. With the boucle and the US size D (3.0mm, Japanese size 5/0) crochet hook, join the motifs at edges with 3-needle bind-off; the schematic suggests the sequence in which to join. For the thumb hole, slip stitch the edges of the motif on each side of the opening. When all motifs have been joined and the arm warmer formed into a tube, pick up from top and bottom edges and work garter stitch in the round along edges.

Arm warmer schematic, shown flat (right arm)

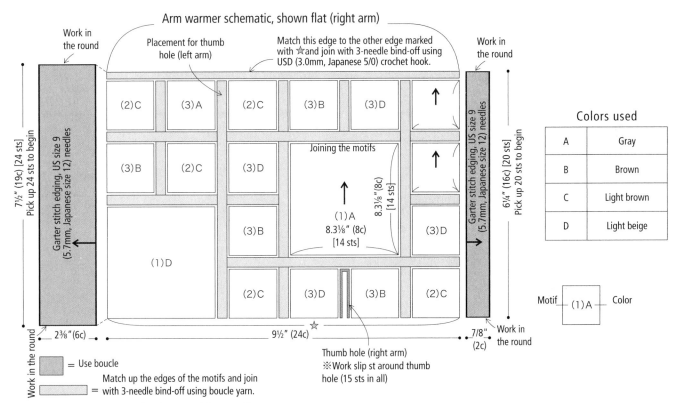

Work in the round

Placement for thumb hole (left arm)

Match this edge to the other edge marked with ☆ and join with 3-needle bind-off using USD (3.0mm, Japanese 5/0) crochet hook.

Work in the round

Garter stitch edging, US size 9 (5.7mm, Japanese size 12) needles
Pick up 24 sts to begin
7½" (19c) [24 sts]

(2)C (3)A (2)C (3)B (3)D

↑
↑

Joining the motifs

(3)B (2)C (3)D

↑

(1)A
8.3⅛" (8c) [14 sts]

8.3⅛" (8c) [14 sts]

(3)D

(1)D

(3)B

(2)C (3)D (3)B (2)C

Garter stitch edging, US size 9 (5.7mm, Japanese size 12) needles
Pick up 20 sts to begin
6¼" (16c) [20 sts]

Work in the round

2⅜" (6c)   9½" (24c)   7/8" (2c)

Work in the round

☆

Thumb hole (right arm)
※Work slip st around thumb hole (15 sts in all)

Colors used

A	Gray
B	Brown
C	Light brown
D	Light beige

Motif — (1)A — Color

■ = Use boucle

▨ = Match up the edges of the motifs and join with 3-needle bind-off using boucle yarn.

※ For the left arm, reverse the placement of the top and bottom garter stitch edges and placement of thumb hole (see schematic).
※ When edging is complete, bind off in purl.

Motifs, using US size 4 (3.6mm, Japanese size 5) needles

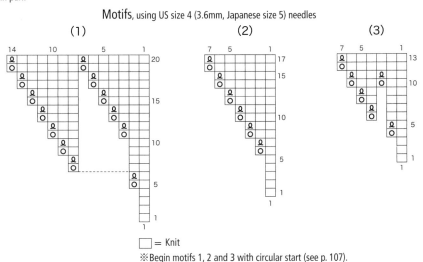

(1)   (2)   (3)

□ = Knit
※ Begin motifs 1, 2 and 3 with circular start (see p. 107).

Fair Isle basket cover P96

Yarn used Puppy Princess Anny
Blue (color 534), 5g
Pink (color 527), 35g
Brown (color 510), 10g
Green (color 536), 10g
Navy blue (color 516), 10g
White (color 502), 35g
Substitution Use DK-weight wool. Yardages:
Blue, 16 yards (15 meters)
Pink, 108 yards (100 meters)
Brown, 32 yards (29 meters)
Green, 32 yards (29 meters)
Navy blue, 32 yards (29 meters)
White, 108 yards (100 meters)

Needles US size 5 (4.2mm, Japanese size 7) circular or double points, crochet hook US size E (3.5mm, Japanese size 6/0) or size to obtain gauge
Finished measurements: circumference at base 25⅝ in (65 cm), top opening circumference 29½ in (75 cm), height 7 in (18 cm).
Gauge in stranded pattern, 24 stitches and 25 rows = 4 in (10 cm)

INSTRUCTIONS

For the body of the cover, use waste yarn and provisional cast-on. Knit in stranded pattern, working increases in rounds 21 and 33 as noted on chart. When complete, bind off with white. Work the crocheted edging. Glue the cover to the basket.

Edging Use pink with US E (3.5mm, Japanese 6/0) crochet hook

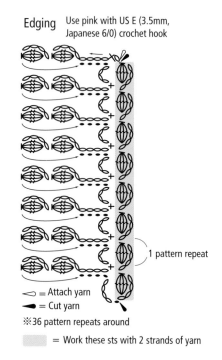

⊂ = Attach yarn
◀ = Cut yarn

※36 pattern repeats around

▨ = Work these sts with 2 strands of yarn

1 pattern repeat

Bag cover

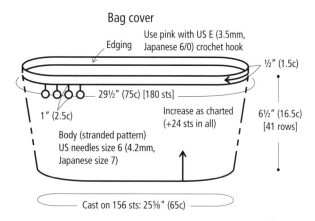

Edging
Use pink with US E (3.5mm, Japanese 6/0) crochet hook
½" (1.5c)
29½" (75c) [180 sts]
1" (2.5c)
Increase as charted (+24 sts in all)
6½" (16.5c) [41 rows]
Body (stranded pattern)
US needles size 6 (4.2mm, Japanese size 7)
Cast on 156 sts: 25⅝" (65c)

Stranded pattern

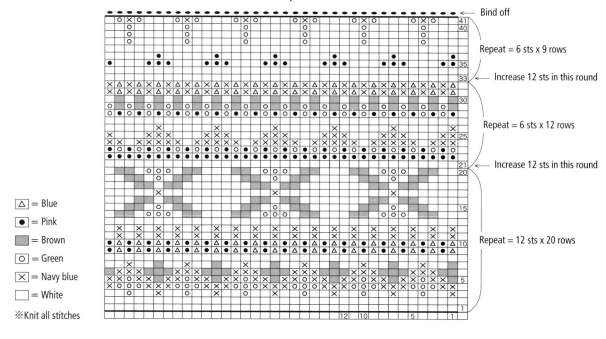

△ = Blue
● = Pink
▨ = Brown
○ = Green
✕ = Navy blue
□ = White

※Knit all stitches

Bind off
Repeat = 6 sts x 9 rows
Increase 12 sts in this round
Repeat = 6 sts x 12 rows
Increase 12 sts in this round
Repeat = 12 sts x 20 rows

※In round 21, make an M1 increase every 13 sts; in round 33, make an M1 increase every 14 sts.

Fringed mittens P97

Yarn used Daruma Prime Merino Worsted
Colors Tan (color 3), 25g
Gray (color 12), 40g
Red (color 13), 20g
Black (color 15), 20g
Substitution Use worsted-weight wool. Yardages:
Tan, 60 yards (55 meters)
Gray, 95 yards (86 meters)
Red, 48 yards (43 meters)
Black, 48 yards (43 meters)
Needles used Double pointed-needles US size 7 (4.5mm, Japanese size 8) or size to obtain gauge
Finished measurements Hand circumference: 7½ in (19 cm)
Length 9¼ in (23.5 cm)
Gauge 22 sts and 27 rows to 4 in (10 cm) in stranded pattern

INSTRUCTIONS

Use waste yarn to cast on provisionally. Work the stranded pattern in the round as charted. Use waste yarn to place the thumb hole where indicated. When complete, graft the last 9 sts on each side to the sts on the other side.

Remove the waste yarn for the thumb hole, pick up the live stitches and work the thumb.

At the cuff edge, remove the provisional cast-on. Working in garter st with gray, tie fringes of each color onto the stitches at 3cm intervals, as illustrated. When garter rows are complete, bind off.

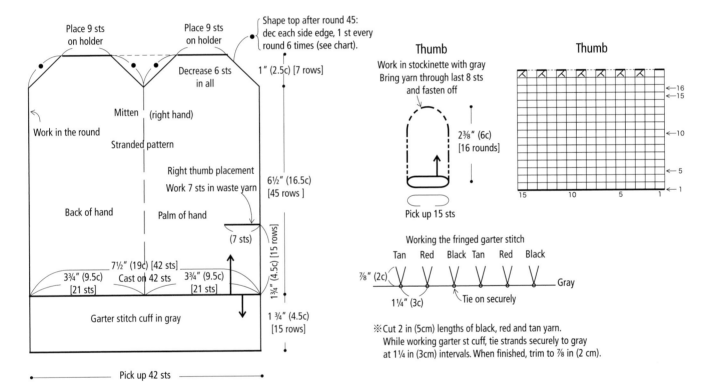

Place 9 sts on holder
Place 9 sts on holder
Shape top after round 45: dec each side edge, 1 st every round 6 times (see chart).
Decrease 6 sts in all
1" (2.5c) [7 rows]
Mitten (right hand)
Work in the round
Stranded pattern
Right thumb placement
Work 7 sts in waste yarn
6½" (16.5c) [45 rows]
Back of hand
Palm of hand
(7 sts)
1¾" (4.5c) [15 rows]
7½" (19c) [42 sts]
3¾" (9.5c) [21 sts]
Cast on 42 sts
3¾" (9.5c) [21 sts]
1¾" (4.5c) [15 rows]
Garter stitch cuff in gray
Pick up 42 sts

※ Use US size 7 (4.5mm, Japanese 8) needle throughout
※ See chart for left thumb placement
☆ See illustration for working fringed garter st

Thumb
Work in stockinette with gray
Bring yarn through last 8 sts and fasten off
2⅜" (6c) [16 rounds]
Pick up 15 sts

Thumb
←16
←15
←10
←5
←1
15   10   5   1

Working the fringed garter stitch
Tan Red Black Tan Red Black
⅞" (2c)
1¼" (3c)
Tie on securely
Gray

※ Cut 2 in (5cm) lengths of black, red and tan yarn.
While working garter st cuff, tie strands securely to gray at 1¼ in (3cm) intervals. When finished, trim to ⅞ in (2 cm).

Stranded pattern

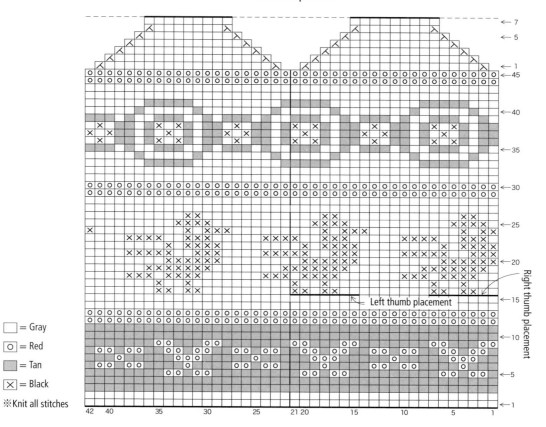

- □ = Gray
- ⊙ = Red
- ▩ = Tan
- ☒ = Black

※Knit all stitches

Right thumb placement

Left thumb placement

White sweater P99

Yarns used Hamanaka Etoffe, white (color 1), 275g
Hamanaka Span Tear white (color 1), 60g
Substitution Use Aran-weight fuzzy alpaca blend:
830 yards (750 meters)
Use laceweight mohair blend yarn with sparkles:
330 yards (300 meters)
Other materials 1 button, ½ in (1.5 cm) in diameter
Needles US sizes 6 and 7 (4.2mm and 4.5mm, Japanese sizes
7 and 8), crochet hook US size H (5.0mm, Japanese size 8/0)
or size to obtain gauge
Finished measurements bust 37¾ in (96 cm); across back
shoulders 14¼ in (36 cm); sleeve length 20⅝ in (52.5 cm)
Gauge in stockinette (with alpaca blend), 15 stitches and 25
rows = 4 in (10 cm); in overall stitch pattern, 23 stitches and 27
rows = 4 in (10 cm)

INSTRUCTIONS

For back, center front, side fronts and sleeves, use waste yarn
and a provisional cast-on. Knit as shown on charts and schematics, using 2 strands of laceweight mohair blend where that yarn
is called for in pattern stitch. Seam side fronts to center front. At
front and back hems and sleeve bottoms, remove the provisional
cast-on, place stitches on a needle, decrease where indicated
and work in garter stitch. Bind off. Join shoulders with 3-needle
bind-off, then sew side and underarm seams.
Pick up stitches for the neckband, beginning at center back and
following neckband chart. Bind off in twisted rib. Crochet the
button loop where indicated. Sew in sleeves.

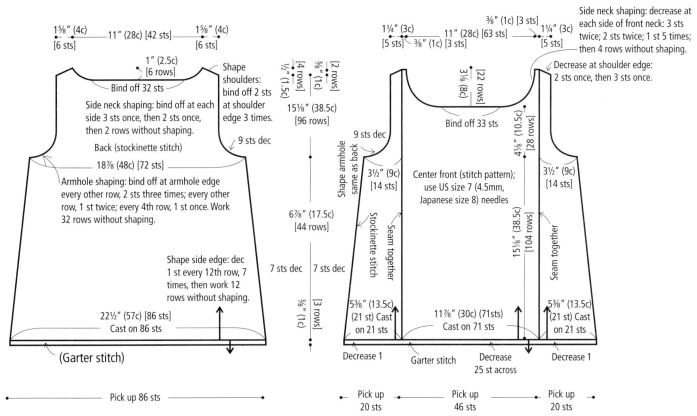

※ Work stockinette in alpaca blend with US size 7
(4.5mm, Japanese size 8) needles.
※ Work garter stitch in alpaca blend with US size 6
(4.2mm, Japanese size 7) needles.

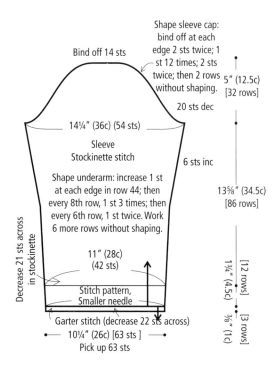

Shape sleeve cap: bind off at each edge 2 sts twice; 1 st 12 times; 2 sts twice; then 2 rows without shaping.

Bind off 14 sts

5" (12.5c) [32 rows]

20 sts dec

14¼" (36c) (54 sts)

Sleeve
Stockinette stitch

6 sts inc

Shape underarm: increase 1 st at each edge in row 44; then every 8th row, 1 st 3 times; then every 6th row, 1 st twice. Work 6 more rows without shaping.

13⅝" (34.5c) [86 rows]

Decrease 21 sts across in stockinette

11" (28c) (42 sts)

Stitch pattern, Smaller needle

1¾" (4.5c) [12 rows]

Garter stitch (decrease 22 sts across)

⅜" (1c) [3 rows]

10¼" (26c) [63 sts]
Pick up 63 sts

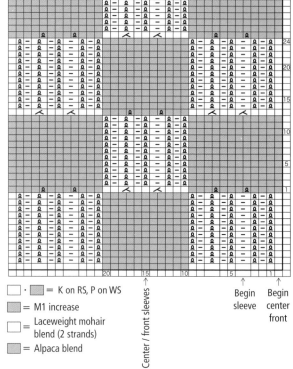

Stranded pattern

One repeat of stitch pattern = 20 sts and 24 rows

Center / front sleeves

Begin sleeve

Begin center front

☐ · ▨ = K on RS, P on WS

▨ = M1 increase

☐ = Laceweight mohair blend (2 strands)

▨ = Alpaca blend

Garter stitch

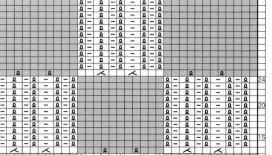

Bind off in purl

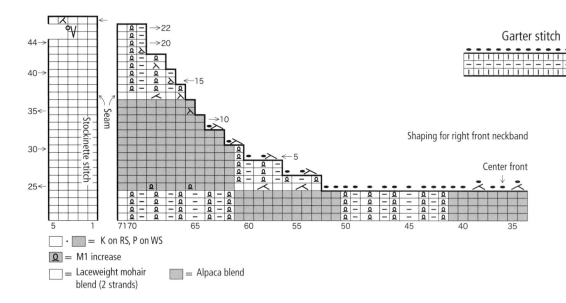

Shaping for right front neckband

Center front

Seam

Stockinette stitch

☐ · ▨ = K on RS, P on WS

Ω = M1 increase

☐ = Laceweight mohair blend (2 strands)

▨ = Alpaca blend

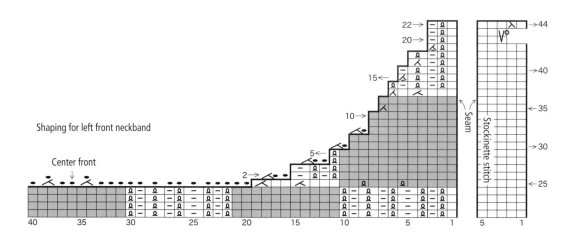

Shaping for left front neckband

Center front

Seam

Stockinette stitch

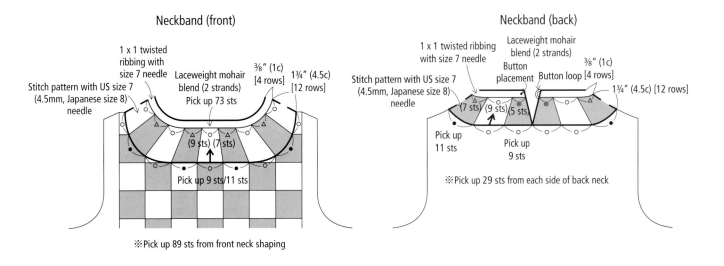

Neckband (front)

Stitch pattern with US size 7 (4.5mm, Japanese size 8) needle

1 x 1 twisted ribbing with size 7 needle

Laceweight mohair blend (2 strands) Pick up 73 sts

⅜" (1c) [4 rows]

1¾" (4.5c) [12 rows]

(9 sts) (7 sts)

Pick up 9 sts/11 sts

※Pick up 89 sts from front neck shaping

Neckband (back)

1 x 1 twisted ribbing with size 7 needle

Laceweight mohair blend (2 strands)

Button placement

Button loop [4 rows]

⅜" (1c)

Stitch pattern with US size 7 (4.5mm, Japanese size 8) needle

1¾" (4.5c) [12 rows]

(7 sts) (9 sts) (5 sts)

Pick up 11 sts

Pick up 9 sts

※Pick up 29 sts from each side of back neck

How to work neckband

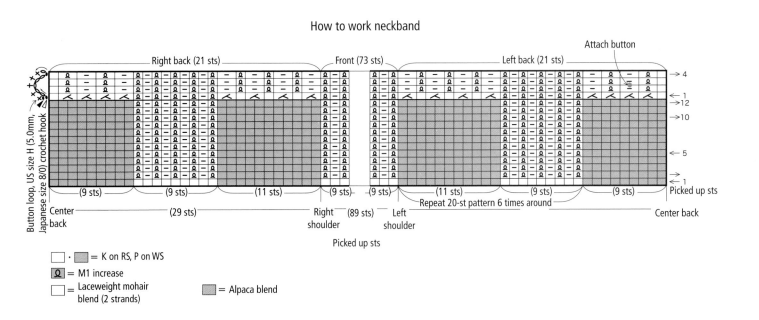

Button loop, US size H (5.0mm, Japanese size 8/0) crochet hook

Right back (21 sts)

Front (73 sts)

Left back (21 sts)

Attach button

→ 4
← 1
→ 12
→ 10
← 5
→ 1
← 1

(9 sts) (9 sts) (11 sts) (9 sts) (9 sts) (11 sts) (9 sts) (9 sts)

Picked up sts

Center back

(29 sts)

Right shoulder

(89 sts)

Left shoulder

Repeat 20-st pattern 6 times around

Center back

Picked up sts

☐ · ▦ = K on RS, P on WS

Ω = M1 increase

☐ = Laceweight mohair blend (2 strands)

▦ = Alpaca blend

Nordic coat P101

Yarn used Ski Menuet, black (color 17), 400g, and beige (color 18), 320g.
Substitution Worsted weight wool.
Yardages Black, 1030 yards (935 meters)
White, 830 yards (745 meters)
Other materials: 2 sets of hook and eye fasteners
Needles US sizes 2 and 6 (3.0mm and 3.9mm, Japanese sizes 3 and 6) or size to obtain gauge
Finished measurements Bust 41¾ in (106 cm), length 28⅛ in (71.5 cm), half-wingspan (center back to cuff) 23¼ in (59 cm)
Gauge in stranded pattern stitch, 21 stitches and 25 rows = 4 in (10 cm)

INSTRUCTIONS

Use a provisional cast-on for body and sleeve sections. Follow the charts. While working row 1 of stranded pattern A, pick up the purl bumps from the provisional cast-on and k2tog with next st on needle to create a doubled hem. Sew the sleeves to front and back, then seam underarms and sides. Pick up sts as indicated from the front, back and tops of sleeves and work the front and neckband pattern as charted. Fold band over and sew in place. Attach ties; sew on hooks and eyes.

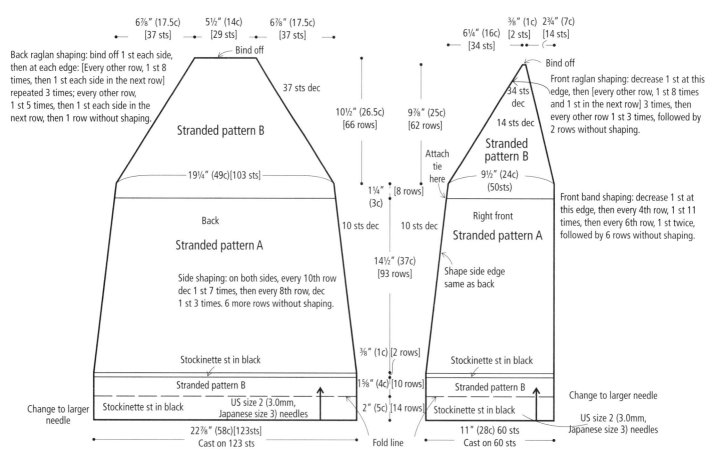

6⅞" (17.5c) [37 sts]   5½" (14c) [29 sts]   6⅞" (17.5c) [37 sts]

Bind off

Back raglan shaping: bind off 1 st each side, then at each edge: [Every other row, 1 st 8 times, then 1 st each side in the next row] repeated 3 times; every other row, 1 st 5 times, then 1 st each side in the next row, then 1 row without shaping.

37 sts dec

Stranded pattern B

19¼" (49c)[103 sts]

10½" (26.5c) [66 rows]

Back

Stranded pattern A

Side shaping: on both sides, every 10th row dec 1 st 7 times, then every 8th row, dec 1 st 3 times. 6 more rows without shaping.

10 sts dec

1¼" (3c) [8 rows]

Stockinette st in black

Stranded pattern B

Stockinette st in black   US size 2 (3.0mm, Japanese size 3) needles

Change to larger needle

22⅞" (58c)[123sts]
Cast on 123 sts

⅜" (1c) [2 rows]
1⅝" (4c) [10 rows]
2" (5c) [14 rows]

Fold line

※ Use US 6 (3.9mm, Japanese size 6) needles unless specified otherwise

---

6¼" (16c) [34 sts]   ⅜" (1c) [2 sts]   2¾" (7c) [14 sts]

Bind off

34 sts dec

Front raglan shaping: decrease 1 st at this edge, then [every other row, 1 st 8 times and 1 st in the next row] 3 times, then every other row 1 st 3 times, followed by 2 rows without shaping.

14 sts dec

Stranded pattern B

9⅞" (25c) [62 rows]

Attach tie here

9½" (24c) (50sts)

Right front

Stranded pattern A

Shape side edge same as back

Front band shaping: decrease 1 st at this edge, then every 4th row, 1 st 11 times, then every 6th row, 1 st twice, followed by 6 rows without shaping.

14½" (37c) [93 rows]

10 sts dec

Stockinette st in black

Stranded pattern B

Change to larger needle

Stockinette st in black

US size 2 (3.0mm, Japanese size 3) needles

11" (28c) 60 sts
Cast on 60 sts

※ Make the left front as a mirror image of the right front.

124

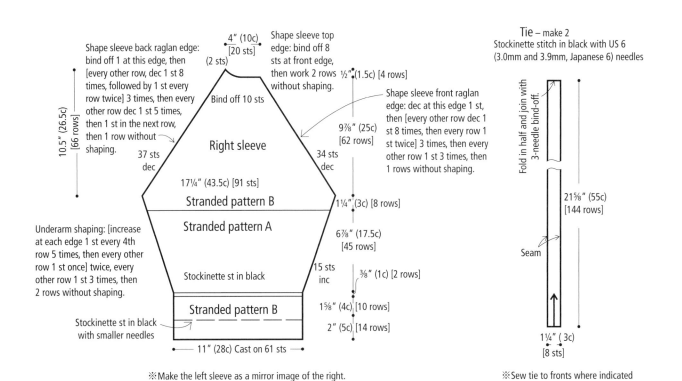

Shape sleeve back raglan edge: bind off 1 at this edge, then [every other row, dec 1 st 8 times, followed by 1 st every row twice] 3 times, then every other row dec 1 st 5 times, then 1 st in the next row, then 1 row without shaping.

10.5" (26.5c) [66 rows]

4" (10c) [20 sts]
(2 sts)

Shape sleeve top edge: bind off 8 sts at front edge, then work 2 rows without shaping.

½" (1.5c) [4 rows]

Shape sleeve front raglan edge: dec at this edge 1 st, then [every other row dec 1 st 8 times, then every row 1 st twice] 3 times, then every other row 1 st 3 times, then 1 rows without shaping.

Bind off 10 sts

Right sleeve

9⅞" (25c) [62 rows]

37 sts dec

34 sts dec

17¼" (43.5c) [91 sts]

Stranded pattern B

1¼" (3c) [8 rows]

Stranded pattern A

6⅞" (17.5c) [45 rows]

Underarm shaping: [increase at each edge 1 st every 4th row 5 times, then every other row 1 st once] twice, every other row 1 st 3 times, then 2 rows without shaping.

Stockinette st in black

15 sts inc

⅜" (1c) [2 rows]

Stranded pattern B

1⅝" (4c) [10 rows]

Stockinette st in black with smaller needles

2" (5c) [14 rows]

11" (28c) Cast on 61 sts

※Make the left sleeve as a mirror image of the right.

Tie – make 2
Stockinette stitch in black with US 6 (3.0mm and 3.9mm, Japanese 6) needles

Fold in half and join with 3-needle bind-off.

21⅝" (55c) [144 rows]

Seam

1¼" (3c) [8 sts]

※Sew tie to fronts where indicated

Stranded stitch patterns

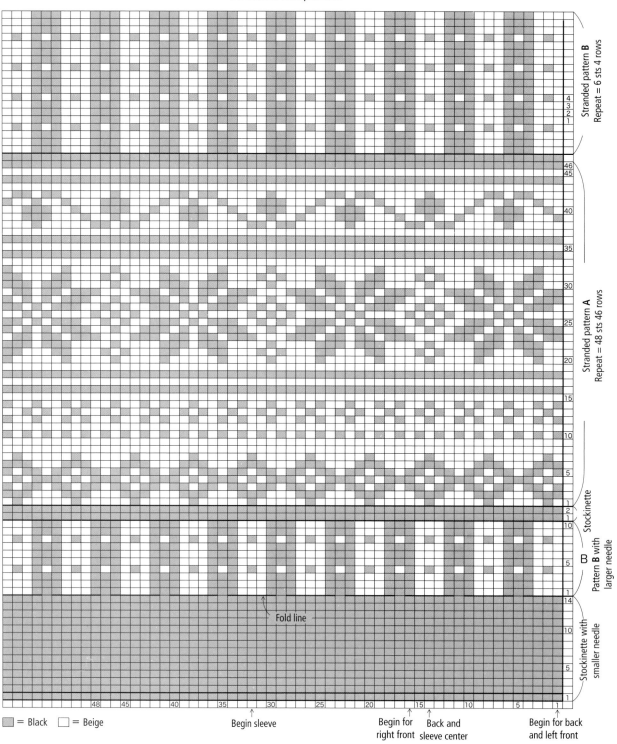

Stranded pattern **B**
Repeat = 6 sts 4 rows

Stranded pattern **A**
Repeat = 48 sts 46 rows

Stockinette

Pattern **B** with larger needle

Stockinette with smaller needle

Fold line

Begin sleeve   Begin for right front   Back and sleeve center   Begin for back and left front

☐ = Black   ☐ = Beige

※ Work all stitches in stockinette
※ To make hem, in row 1 of stranded pattern A, pick up the purl bump from behind the stitch in row 1 and k2tog with the next st on LN. Alternately, fold up and sew in place after knitting is complete.

Front and neck band: see chart below

US sizes 2 and 6 (3.0mm and 3.9mm,
Japanese sizes 3 and 6) needles

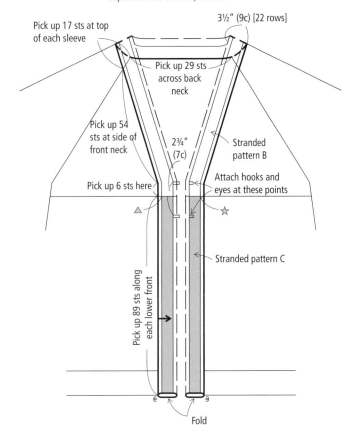

Pick up 17 sts at top of each sleeve

3½" (9c) [22 rows]

Pick up 29 sts across back neck

Pick up 54 sts at side of front neck

2¾" (7c)

Stranded pattern B

Pick up 6 sts here

Attach hooks and eyes at these points

Stranded pattern C

Pick up 89 sts along each lower front

Fold

Chart for front and neck band

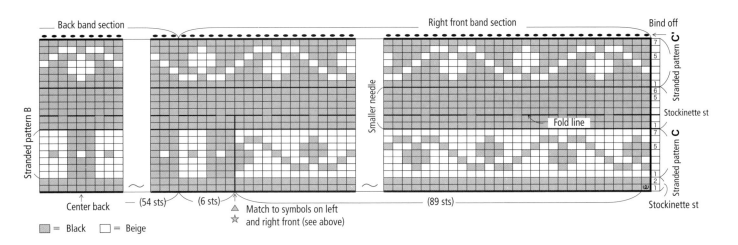

Back band section

Right front band section

Bind off

Stranded pattern B

Center back

(54 sts)

(6 sts)

△ Match to symbols on left
☆ and right front (see above)

Smaller needle

Stranded pattern C

Fold line

Stockinette st

Stranded pattern C

Stockinette st

(89 sts)

▨ = Black   ☐ = Beige

※All sts in stockinette
※Make the neck and front bands mirror image from center back.
※After binding off, whip stitch the bound-off edge to the back of the row of picked up sts.
※Use US 6 (3.9mm, Japanese size 6) needle except for black rows 1-6

Symbol Directory

This directory defines most of the stitch symbols used in the book, cross-referenced to the stitch patterns in which they appear. You'll find definitions in three places:

- For symbols with a page reference, turn to the page for a step-by-step illustration.
- For symbols without a page reference, a definition is included in this table.
- For some of the more complex symbols, especially those that are used in only one stitch pattern, you'll find a definition near the appropriate chart. Many of these are variations on the basic stitches.

If the stitch is worked on both right side and wrong side, both definitions are provided. If "WS" is not specified, the stitch is only used on the RS.

A number of these patterns have multiple colors, and the color key appears next to the chart.

Abbreviations used in this section

RN = Right needle
LN = Left needle
St = Stitch
K = Knit
P = Purl
YO = Yarn over
St = Stitch
Ktbl = Knit through the back loop
Ptbl = Purl through the back loop
Sl = slip
Wyib = with yarn in back of work
Wyif = with yarn in front
K2tog = Knit 2 together
K2togtbl = Knit 2 together through the back loops
P2tog = Purl 2 together
P2togtbl = Purl 2 together through the back loops
Psso = pass slipped stitch over
SKP = Slip 1 knitwise, knit 1, pass slipped stitch over
SSK = [Slip 1 knitwise] twice, return 2 st to LN, k2togtbl.
SSP = [slip 1 knitwise] twice, slip 2 stitches back to LN, then p2togtbl. See p.137 for alternate method,
    see p. 137 for alternate method.
M1 = Make one: with tip of RN, pick up the strand of yarn before the next stitch on LN and ktbl
CN = cable needle
K1 below = insert RN into the stitch below the next st on LN and k, letting the next st on LN drop down

Symbol	How to knit it	Illustrated on page	Used in stitch pattern(s)
	RS: K WS: P	136	Most
	RS: P WS: K	136	Most

Symbol	How to knit it	Illustrated on page	Used in stitch pattern(s)
	Twisted knit st: RS: Ktbl WS: Ptbl Note: This symbol is also used for the M1 increase.	136	Many
	Twisted purl: Ptbl	136	144
	Yarnover: RS: YO WS: YO	136	Many
	YO, SKP or SSK	136	Many
	K2tog, yo	136	Many
	SSK: RS: SKP or SSK WS: P2togtbl or SSP	137	Many
	K2tog: RS: K2tog WS: P2tog	137	Many
	P2tog: tbl or SSP	137	41, 145
	RS: P2tog WS: K2tog	137	15, 41, 133, 145, 146
	Centered double decrease (CDD) RS: Sl 2 tog knitwise, k1, p2sso. WS: Switch positions of sts ① and ② so st ① is in front of st ②, then p3tog.	137	7, 40, 41, 46, 89, 93, 122, 123, 124, 128, 147, 150
	Centered quadruple decrease (CQD)	137	50, 53, 101, 144, 148
	K5tog: knit 5 tog		10, 23, 40
	[Sl 1 knitwise] 4 times, k1, p4sso		36, 125, 130
	Left double dec (sk2p)	138	42, 43, 50, 125, 127, 128, 129, 143
	Right double dec (k3tog)	138	40, 43, 50, 52, 89, 112, 143
	Work k1, p1 into the same st		61, 126

Symbol	How to knit it	Illustrated on page	Used in stitch pattern(s)
	Right lifted increase	138	
	Left lifted increase	138	
	Make 3 knit sts from 1: k, yo, k into 1 st	138	12, 40, 41, 52, 89, 112, 127, 128, 129, 150
	Make 3 purl sts from 1: p, yo, p into 1 st	138	
	Make 5 knit sts from 1: k, yo, k, yo, k into 1 st		10, 36, 40, 53, 101, 148 23 (9-st version)
	Cross 1 to left	139	8, 19, 39, 94, 100, 101, 103, 106, 125
	Cross 1 to right	139	24, 39, 100, 101, 103, 105, 106, 125, 133
	Cross 1 to left over purl	139	94, 103, 105
	Cross 1 to right over purl	139	94, 103, 105
	Place 2 sts on CN, hold to front, p1; k2 from CN		96, 101
	Place 1 st on CN, hold to back, k2; p1 from CN		96, 101
	Cross ktbl to the left	139	37
	Cross ktbl to the right	139	37
	Cross ktbl to the left over purl	140	99, 101, 112
	Cross ktbl to the right over purl	140	99, 101, 112
	Place 1 st on CN, hold to front, place 1 st on another CN, hold to back; k1; p1 from back CN, ktbl from front CN		101
	1-over-2 cross to left Place 1 st on CN, hold to front, k2; k1 from CN		1, 104
	1-over-2 cross to right Place 2 sts on CN, hold to back, k1; k2 from CN		104

Symbol	How to knit it	Illustrated on page	Used in stitch pattern(s)
	Place 1 st on CN, hold to front, p2; k1 from CN		104, 108
	Place 2 sts on CN, hold to back, k1; p2 from CN		104, 108
	Place 1 st on CN, hold to front; place 1 st on another CN, hold to back; k1, p1 from back CN, k1 from front CN		107
	Place 1 st on CN, hold to back; place 1 st on another CN, hold to back; k1, p1 from second CN, k1 from first CN		105, 107
	Cable 2 to left	140	97, 100, 101, 109, 146
	Cable 2 to right	140	100, 101, 109, 146
	Place 2 sts on CN, hold to front, p2; k2 from CN		96, 146
	Place 2 sts on CN, hold to back, k2; p2 from CN		96, 146
	Place 1 st on CN, hold to front; place 2 sts on CN, hold to back; k1, p2 from back CN, k1 from front CN		103
	Place 1 st on CN, hold to back; place 2 sts on CN, hold to back; k1, p2 from second CN, k1 from first CN		103
	2-over-3 cable to the right with center purl	140	
	2-over-3 cable to the left with center purl	140	
	Place 3 sts on CN, hold to front, k2; k3 from CN		106
	Place 2 sts on CN, hold to back, k3; k2 from CN		106
	Place 3 sts on CN, hold to front, p2; k3 from CN		106
	Place 2 sts on CN, hold to back, k3; p2 from CN		106

Symbol	How to knit it	Illustrated on page	Used in stitch pattern(s)
	Place 3 sts on CN, hold to front, k3; k3 from CN		44, 92, 100, 103, 106, 108, 109
	Place 3 sts on CN, hold to back, k3; k3 from CN		92, 100, 103, 108
	Place 4 sts on CN, hold to front, k4; k4 from CN		98, 135
	Place 4 sts on CN, hold to back, k4; k4 from CN		98, 122, 135
	Pass 1 st to left	141	22
	Pass 1 st to right	141	
	Cross 3 through to left: Sl 6 sts from LN to RN, dropping the extra wraps. Insert tip of LN into the first 3 sts, from left to right, and lift them over the second set of 3, but don't drop them. Return all sts to LN and k6.		20 21 (5-over-5 version)
	Cross 3 through to right: Sl 6 sts from LN to RN, dropping the extra wraps. Return all sts to LN. Insert tip of LN into sts ④, ⑤ and ⑥, from right to left, and lift them over sts ①, ② and ③, leaving them on LN; k6.		20 21 (5-over-5 version)
	Knot st to left	141	
	Knot st to right	141	99
	Brioche stitch with knit	141	54, 55, 131, 132
	Brioche stitch with purl	141	131, 132
	Lifted knit st 2 rows below	142	47, 49, 57, 89, 123

Symbol	How to knit it	Illustrated on page	Used in stitch pattern(s)
← ○ ⇒ ← ● ⇒ ×	Lifted purl st 2 rows below	142	145 (over 2 rows)
3	3-stitch, 3-row bobble	142	
5	5-stitch, 5-row bobble	142	101 (3-row version)
← ● ⇒ ×	Slip a knit st	142	13, 47, 49, 50, 103, 118, 121, 139, 150 48 (over 3 rows) 51, 17 (over 4 rows) 63 (over 12 rows)
	Slip slip 1 purl st wyib (same as slipping a k st)		139 118 (over 3 rows) 64 (over 4 rows)
	Stitch pulled out to right	142	106 (over 5 sts)
3	3-st wrapped knot	143	
	E-wrap cast on Put a backward loop (e-wrap) on LN	143	16, 54, 61, 116, 119, 140
2	Double-wrapped knit st RS: k, wrapping yarn twice around needle. WS: p, wrapping yarn twice around needle.	143	20, 36, 51, 118, 128, 129
3	Triple-wrapped knit st RS: k, wrapping yarn three times around needle. WS: p, wrapping yarn three times around needle.	143	21 44 (4 wraps)
→ ● ← → ← → ← → ×	Tuck stitch with lifted purl bump	143	63, 114 (over 4 rows) and 9 rows); 115 (over 14 rows)

Symbol	How to knit it	Illustrated on page	Used in stitch pattern(s)
	Slanted tuck stitch	143	115, 117 (over 3 rows)
	Bind off		16, 61, 66, 68, 84, 85, 86, 88, 89, 90, 121, 123, 126, 127
Crochet stitches			
	Chain st		43 123 (ch 3) 127, 130 (ch 7) 128 (ch 5)
	Single crochet		66, 68, 128, 129, 130
	Single crochet through back loop only		84, 86
	Bind off with decrease: insert needle through two sts at the same time and bind off		85, 89, 121
	Picot: Insert crochet hook into next st on LN, pull out a loop, and chain 3. Slip st the last chain to the first chain, and move st to RN.		66, 68, 84, 86, 126
	2 HDC bobble: Insert crochet hook into next st on LN, chain 2, [yarn over hook, pull up another loop in the same place] twice (5 loops on hook), yarn over hook and pull through all loops. Move st to RN.		92
	3 HDC bobble: Insert crochet hook into next st on LN, pull up a loop (approx. 2 chains long), [yarn over hook, pull up another loop in the same place] three times (7 loops on hook), yarn over hook and pull through all loops. Move st to RN.		146

Symbol	How to knit it	Illustrated on page	Used in stitch pattern(s)
	2 DC bobble: Insert crochet hook into next st on LN, chain 2; [yarn over hook, pull up a loop in the same place, pull yarn through 2 loops] twice; pull yarn through all loops. Move st to RN.		106
	2 DC bobble: Insert crochet hook into next st on LN, chain 3; [yarn over hook, pull up a loop in the same place, pull yarn through 2 loops] twice; pull yarn through all loops. Move st to RN.		91
	3 DC bobble: Insert crochet hook into next st on LN, chain 2; [yarn over hook, pull up a loop in the same place, pull yarn through 2 loops] three times; pull yarn through all loops. Move st to RN.		93
	3 DC bobble: Insert crochet hook into next st on LN, chain 3; [yarn over hook, pull up a loop in the same place, pull yarn through 2 loops] three times; pull yarn through all loops, ch1. Move st to RN.		95
	4 DC bobble: Insert crochet hook into next st on LN, chain 3; [yarn over hook, pull up a loop in the same place, pull yarn through 2 loops] four times; pull yarn through all loops. Move st to RN.		94

Knitting Basics

⊞ Knit

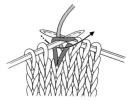

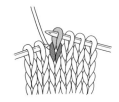

❶ Insert RN into next st on LN from front to back, wrap yarn over RN as shown and bring it through.

❷ Drop st off LN. One knit st complete.

⊟ Purl

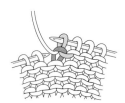

❶ Insert RN into next st on LN from back to front, wrap yarn over RN as shown and bring it through.

❷ Drop st off LN. One purl st complete.

⊡ Twisted knit st

❶ Insert RN into back loop of next st on LN as shown.

❷ Wrap yarn over RN and bring it through.

⊡ Twisted purl st

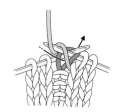

❶ Insert RN into back loop of next st on LN as shown in the direction of the arrow.

❷ Wrap yarn over RN and bring it through.

○ Yarnover (yo)

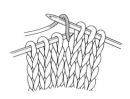

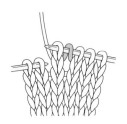

❶ From front, wrap yarn over RN as shown.

❷ Knit the next st. Yarnover makes an increase.

╲○ Yarnover, skp

Yarnover, then skp the next two sts on LN.

○╱ K2tog, yarnover

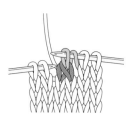

K2tog the next 2 sts on LN, then yarnover.

◻ SKP

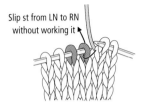 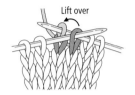

❶ Insert RN into next st on LN as if to knit, slip it to RN.

❷ Knit next st on LN, use tip of LN to pass slipped st over it as shown.

◻ K2tog

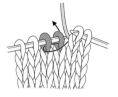 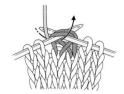

❶ Insert RN knitwise into next 2 sts on LN together,

❷ Wrap yarn over RN and knit both together.

◻ SSP

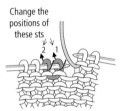 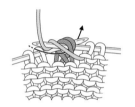

❶ Change the positions of the next 2 sts on LN so that st 1 crosses to the left over st 2.

❷ Insert RN through both purlwise, wrap yarn over RN and bring it through both.

◻ P2tog

 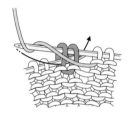

❶ Insert RN into next 2 sts on LN together.

❷ Wrap yarn over RN and bring it through both.

◻ Centered double decrease (CDD)

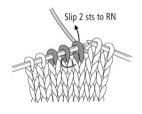 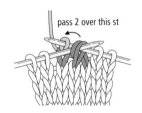

❶ Insert RN into next 2 sts on LN together knitwise as shown and slip both to RN.

❷ Knit next st on LN, then pass 2 slipped sts over together.

RS: Follow steps 1 and 2. WS: Switch positions of sts ① and ② so st ① is in front of st ②, then p3tog.

◻ Centered quadruple decrease (CQD)

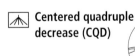 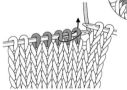 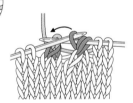

❶ Insert RN into next 3 sts on LN together knitwise, as shown, and slip all 3 to RN.

❷ K2tog the next 2 sts on LN, then pass the 2 slipped sts over together.

⊠ Left double dec (sk2p)

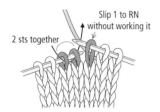

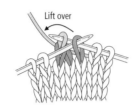

❶ Slip 1 st purlwise from LN to RN without working it.

❷ K2tog the next 2 sts on LN, the pass slipped st over.

⊠ Right double dec (k3tog)

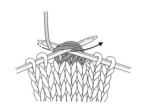

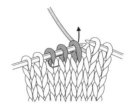

❶ Insert RN knitwise into next 3 sts on LN together.

❷ Wrap yarn over RN and knit 3 together.

⊞ Right lifted increase

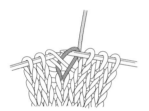

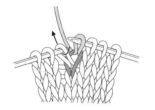

❶ With tip of RN, pick up the right leg of st in the row below next st on LN.

❷ Knit lifted stitch, then the next st on LN. 1 lifted increase completed.

⊞ Left lifted increase

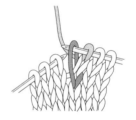

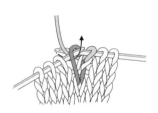

❶ Knit 1 st, then with tip of LN, pick up the left leg of st 2 rows below new st.

❷ Knit lifted st. 1 lifted increase completed.

Make 3 knit sts from 1

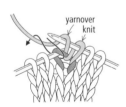

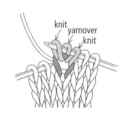

❶ Knit 1, do not remove from LN, yarnover, knit same st again.

❷ 1 st has become 3 sts = double inc complete.

Make 3 purl sts from 1

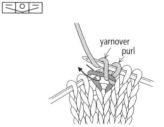

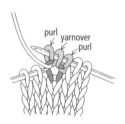

❶ Purl 1, do not remove from LN, yarnover, purl same st again.

❷ 1 st has become 3 sts = double inc complete.

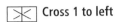 **Cross 1 to left**

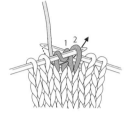 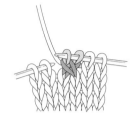

❶ Insert tip of RN from the back into second st on LN and k, without removing from LN.

❷ K 1st st on LN and move both to RN.

Cross 1 to right

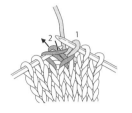 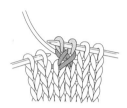

❶ Insert tip of RN from the front into second st on LN and k, without removing from LN.

❷ K 1st st on LN and move both to RN.

Cross 1 to left over purl

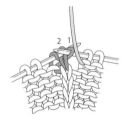 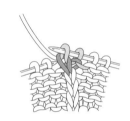

❶ Insert tip of RN from the back into second st on LN and p, without removing from LN.

❷ K 1st st on LN and move both to RN.

Cross 1 to right over purl

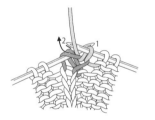 

❶ Insert tip of RN from the front into second st on LN and k, without removing from LN.

❷ P 1st st on LN and move both to RN.

Cross ktbl to the left

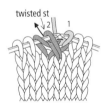 

twisted st

❶ Insert tip of RN from the back into second st on LN and k, without removing from LN.

❷ Ktbl 1st st on LN and move both to RN.

Cross ktbl to the right

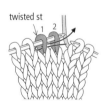 

twisted st

❶ Insert tip of RN from the front into second st on LN and ktbl, without removing from LN.

❷ K 1st st on LN and move both to RN.

Cross ktbl to the left over purl

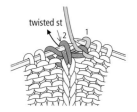

❶ Insert tip of RN from the back into second st on LN and p, without removing from LN.

❷ Ktbl 1st st on LN and move both to RN.

Cross ktbl to the right over purl

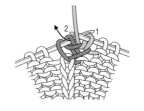

❶ Insert tip of RN from the front into second st on LN and ktbl, without removing from LN.

❷ P 1st st on LN and move both to RN.

4-stitch cable to the left

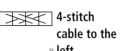

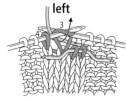

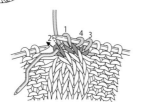

❶ Place 2 sts on CN and hold to front. K2.

❷ k2 from CN.

4-stitch cable to the right

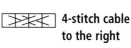

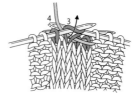

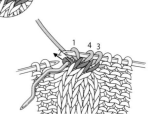

❶ Place 2 sts on CN and hold to back. K2.

❷ K2 from CN.

2-over-3 cable to the left with center purl

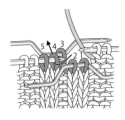

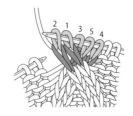

❶ Place 2 sts on CN, hold to front. Place next st on another CN, hold to back.

❷ K2, then p1 from 2nd CN, k2 from first CN.

2-over-3 cable to the right with center purl

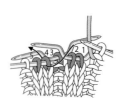

❶ Place 2 sts on CN, hold to back. Place next st on another CN, hold to back.

❷ K2, then p1 from second CN, k2 from first CN.

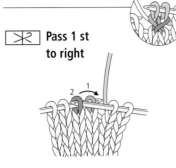

⊠	Pass 1 st to left

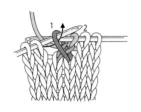

❶ Slip 2 sts to RN purlwise, then use tip of LN to lift the first st over the second (with out dropping it) and replace both on LN.

❷ K both sts in their new positions.

⊠	Pass 1 st to right

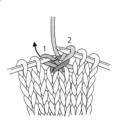

❶ With tip of RN, lift 2nd st over first st on LN (without dropping it).

❷ K both sts in their new positions.

| C | O | I | | **Knot st to left** |

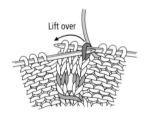

Lift over

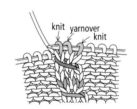

knit yarnover knit

❶ Slip 3 sts to RN purlwise. With tip of LN, lift the 1st st over the other 2 and let it drop. Slip rem 2 sts back to LN.

❷ K, yo, K.

| I | O | D | | **Knot st to right** |

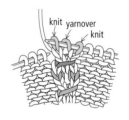

Lift over

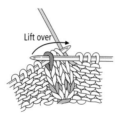

knit yarnover knit

❶ With tip of RN, lift 3rd st on LN over the first 2 and let it drop.

❷ K, yo, k.

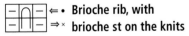 ⇐ • Brioche rib, with
⇒ × brioche st on the knits

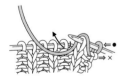

❶ Without working it, slip the k st to RN purlwise, at the same time laying the yarn over the st as shown. P next st.

❷ On the WS row, p the slipped st tog with the strand of yarn over it.

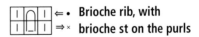 ⇐ • Brioche rib, with
⇒ × brioche st on the purls

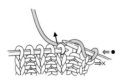

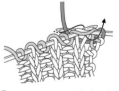

❶ Without working it, slip the p st to RN purlwise, at the same time laying the yarn over the st as shown. K next st.

❷ On the WS row, k the slipped st tog with the strand of yarn over it.

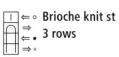 Brioche knit st
 3 rows

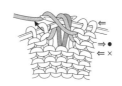
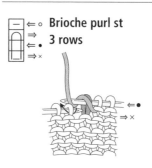

❶ Lay the yarn over RN as shown, front to back, and slip the 1st st knitwise.

❷ On the next row, lay the yarn over RN as shown, front to" back, and slip the sl st from previous row and the strand of yarn over it to RN. P next st. On final row, k all strands (insert).

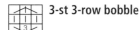 Brioche purl st
3 rows

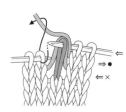

❶ Slip 1st st purlwise, then lay the yarn over RN as shown, front to back. Purl next st.

❷ On the next row, lay the yarn over RN as shown, front to back, and slip the sl st from previous rowand the strand of yarn over it to RN. K next st. On final row, p all strands (inset).

3-st 3-row bobble

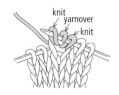

❶ Work k, yo, k into the next st. Turn, p 3.

❷ Turn, work CDD (see p. 137)

5 st 5–row bobble

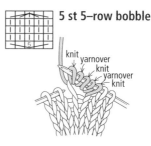
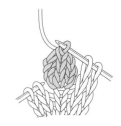

❶ Work k, yo, k, yo, k into the next st. Turn, p5. Turn, k5. Turn, p5.

❷ Turn, k5. Turn, p5. Work CQD (see p. 137).

Slip st

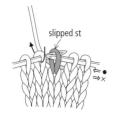
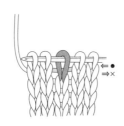

❶ With yarn in back, slip 1 st purlwise.

❷ One slip st completed.

Stitch pulled out to right

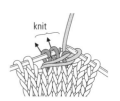

❶ Insert tip of RN into the space between sts ③ and ④ on LN, and pull out a loop. Briefly remove the loop from RN and insert tip of RN the other way into loop and next st on LN.

❷ K2tog the loop and first st, k2.

3-st wrapped knot

❶ K3, place these 3 sts on CN, and wrap working yarn around them 3 times counterclockwise.

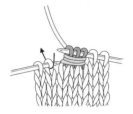

❷ Slip 3 wrapped sts to RN and continue.

 Backward loop (e-wrap)

Right

Left

On knit side, with working yarn, wrap yarn around index finger and put this loop on RN. Tug to tighten.

On purl side, with working yarn, wrap yarn around index finger and put this loop on RN. Tug to tighten.

Double-wrapped knit st

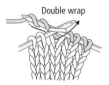 **Double wrap**

Double wrap

Remove from LN

❶ On knit side, insert RN into next st, wrap yarn twice around RN, and bring through the st.

❷ On purl side, insert RN as if to purl, wrap yarn twice around RN, and bring both loops through the st.

Triple-wrapped knit st

 Triple wrap

Triple wrap

Remove from LN

❶ Insert RN into next st, wrap yarn three times around RN, and bring through the st.

❷ On purl side, insert RN as if to purl, wrap yarn three times around RN, and bring both loops through the st.

Tuck stitch (from 6 rows below)

Tuck stitch with lifted purl bump

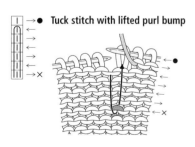

❶ On WS (row marked with black dot), slip next st to RN. Insert tip of LN into purl bump, from top to bottom, 6 rows below st on RN. Lift this loop up and onto LN.

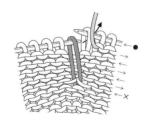

❷ Return slipped st to LN.

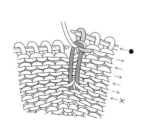

❸ P2tog slipped st with lifted loop.

Slanted tuck stitch (from 5 rows below)

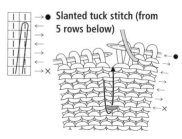

On WS (row marked with black dot), slip next st to RN. Insert tip of LN, from top to bottom, into downward-facing purl bump between these sts 6 rows below. Lift this loop up and onto LN. Slip one st back to LN and p2tog with loop.

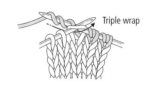

Published by Tuttle Publishing, an imprint of Periplus Editions (HK) Ltd.

www.tuttlepublishing.com

Sozai to Iro de Tanoshimu Boubariami no Moyou 150 sen (NV70125)
Copyright © Keiko Okamoto/NIHON VOGUE-SHA 2012
Photographer: Yoko Kimura, Kana Watanabe, Hitomi Takahashi
All rights reserved.
English translation rights arranged with NIHON VOGUE Corp.
through Japan UNI Agency, Inc., Tokyo
Translated from Japanese by Gayle Roehm

ISBN 978-4-8053-1484-5

Designer Keiko Okamoto
Knitting production team Sayuri Idomoto, Miyoko Kasagawa, Satomi Kashihara, Noriko Kido, Fumie Kojima, Sugako Saeki, Emiko Suzuki, Kanae Seino, Miyuki Tsuchitani, Yoshiko Nakagawa, Etsuko Nakajima, Chihoko Na-kamura, Hisako Hariguchi, Satako Hibi, Kazue Matsuoka, Chikako Matsutomi, Etsuko Matsubara, Hiroko Miyamoto, Mayumi Miyamoto, Akiko Yano, Yukie Yamazaki
Book Design Washizu Design Office
Photography Hitoshi Takahashi ,Yoko Kimura, Watanabe Kana
Styling Tomomi Enai
Diagrams Yumiko Matsumoto
Editorial assistance L & B, Shoko Ishihara, Michiko Enomura
Editing Nihon Vogue, Toshie Yano, Motoko Usami

Distributed by

North America, Latin America & Europe
Tuttle Publishing
364 Innovation Drive, North Clarendon,
VT 05759-9436 U.S.A.
Tel: 1 (802) 773-8930
Fax: 1 (802) 773-6993
info@tuttlepublishing.com
www.tuttlepublishing.com

Japan
Tuttle Publishing
Yaekari Building, 3rd Floor
5-4-12 Osaki, Shinagawa-ku, Tokyo 141 0032
Tel: (81) 3 5437-0171; Fax: (81) 3 5437-0755
sales@tuttle.co.jp; www.tuttle.co.jp

Asia Pacific
Berkeley Books Pte. Ltd.
3 Kallang Sector, #04-01/02,
Singapore 349278
Tel: (65) 67412178
Fax: (65) 67412179
inquiries@periplus.com.sg
www.tuttlepublishing.com

Printed in China   1902RR
22 21 20 19   10 9 8 7 6 5 4 3 2 1

About Tuttle "Books to Span the East and West"

Our core mission at Tuttle Publishing is to create books which bring people together one page at a time. Tuttle was founded in 1832 in the small New England town of Rutland, Vermont (USA). Our fundamental values remain as strong today as they were then—to publish best-in-class books informing the English-speaking world about the countries and peoples of Asia. The world has become a smaller place today and Asia's economic, cultural and political influence has expanded, yet the need for meaningful dialogue and information about this diverse region has never been greater. Since 1948, Tuttle has been a leader in publishing books on the cultures, arts, cuisines, languages and literatures of Asia. Our authors and photographers have won numerous awards and Tuttle has published thousands of books on subjects ranging from martial arts to paper crafts. We welcome you to explore the wealth of information available on Asia at **www.tuttlepublishing.com.**